OCCUPY

12 INSPIRATIONAL STORIES TO AWAKEN THE DREAMER WITHIN, EMPOWERING YOU TO OCCUPY YOUR DESTINY IN LIFE!

COMPILED BY

KISHMA A. GEORGE

Occupy © March 2025
Compiled by Dr. Kishma A. George
Published in the United States of America by
ChosenButterflyPublishing LLC

www.ChosenButterflyPublishing.com

ISBN: 978-1-945377-97-6
First Edition Printing
Printed in the United States of America
March 2025

Table of Contents

The Call to Occupy

By Dr. Kishma A. George

First and foremost, I want to thank you for purchasing this book. Whether you picked it up out of curiosity, to support a co-author, or a deep desire for encouragement, I believe that it is no accident that you are here. *Occupy* is more than just a collection of stories—it is a call to action, a testimony of God's faithfulness, and a powerful reminder that no matter what life throws at us, we are still standing because of His grace.

Each story in this book is woven with pain, perseverance, and ultimate victory. These are real testimonies from men and women who have endured storms that should have broken them—storms of rejection, trauma, disappointment, and loss. Yet, through God's restoration, they now stand as living proof that He can take the broken pieces of our lives and transform them into something beautiful.

I am honored to serve as the visionary for this book, but the true impact comes from the incredible contributors who have shared their journeys with transparency and boldness. Through their stories, you will see the power of faith in action, the strength that comes from trusting God, and the resilience required to **occupy until Jesus returns.**

Occupy Until He Comes – The Call to Stand Firm

From the very beginning, God has called us to occupy—to take authority, to stand in our purpose, and to fulfill the assignments He has given us until the day of Christ's return. In Luke 19:13, Jesus commands, *"Occupy till I come."* This is not a passive calling. It is a divine mandate to actively engage in Kingdom work, using our testimonies, gifts, and experiences to glorify God and edify His people.

As I reflect on the powerful stories shared in this book, I see a recurring theme—God's faithfulness in the midst of struggle, His restoration in the face of brokenness, and His purpose shining through even the darkest seasons. Each author in this compilation has lived through trials that could have silenced them, yet they chose to occupy their broken places, their pain, and their victories, standing firm in their faith.

Broken, Yet Called

Annette Watson-Johnson's story reminds us that our wellness—mental, physical, and spiritual—is crucial to occupying effectively. God does not call us to pour from an empty vessel. Through her testimony, we see how God not only healed her but also equipped her to help others walk in their healing. Her obedience led to the birth of Just Get Well Sea Moss, a business rooted in divine instruction. She reminds us that when we seek God for clarity, He provides wisdom, strategy, and the ability to restore not just ourselves but others.

We are also reminded through Dr. LaTasha Stanley that education is a tool of restoration. God has given us knowledge and wisdom not just for personal advancement but for Kingdom impact. Her journey from being a teenage mother to earning her doctorate is proof that God redeems time. She occupied her struggles and turned them into a testimony that now inspires others to pursue their God-given destiny.

Danielle N. Hall's story is one of breaking the chains of past trauma and allowing God to rewrite the narrative. Through V.O.I.C.E., she is now using her testimony to help other women walk in victory. This is what it means to occupy—to stand in our truth, to refuse to let shame silence us, and to use what the enemy meant for evil as a tool for deliverance.

Then there is the raw, heart-wrenching testimony of a young girl born into a storm, struggling with rejection, colorism, and self-worth. Her journey of finding peace, acceptance, and love through her stepfather reminds us that God always provides what we need, even when it doesn't come in the way we expect. She occupied her broken places, and God brought healing in His perfect time.

Why We Must Occupy Until Jesus Returns

To **occupy** means to be **steadfast, immovable, always abounding in the work of the Lord (1 Corinthians 15:58)**. This means we cannot afford to live in **fear, complacency, or silence**. Too many have been trapped by shame, abuse, and self-doubt, but God is calling His people to **rise up and reclaim their place**.

We must **occupy our faith** by remaining anchored in God's promises, trusting that His Word is true even when our circumstances seem uncertain.

We must **occupy our families**, breaking generational curses and speaking life over our children, marriages, and communities.

We must **occupy our purpose**, refusing to let setbacks define us. Whether it's through business, education, ministry, or advocacy, we must step into what God has ordained for us.

We must **occupy our testimonies**, sharing them boldly so that others can find healing, hope, and the courage to step into their own destiny.

Most importantly, we must occupy until Jesus comes. He is returning for a Church that is active, engaged, and walking in authority. The enemy would love for us to sit in defeat, but we are called to be warriors, to be the light, and to take dominion.

What Will You Do With Your Assignment?

This book is not just a collection of testimonies—it is a declaration that we will not be silenced. Each chapter represents a life that has been transformed, restored, and positioned for impact. Now, the question is:

What will you do with your story?

Will you shrink back, or will you occupy? Will you allow fear to keep you from moving forward, or will you take hold of everything God has promised?

This is not the season to sit still. **This is the time to rise, to stand, to fight, and to occupy—until He comes.**

Thank you for allowing us to walk this journey with you. Now, let's take our place. Let's rise. Let's occupy.

Dr. Kishma's Acknowledgements

First and foremost, I want to give God all the glory and honor, as He made this vision possible. I love You, Lord, with all my heart! ♥ In memory of my beloved father, Edmond Felix George; I am thankful for his encouragement and inspiring me to dream. ♥ To the best mother in the world, Novita Scatliffe-George; I thank you for your love, support, encouraging words and praying for me. Thank you for not giving up on me. I love you, Mom! ♥ To my wonderful daughter Kiniquá, I love you dearly. Thank you for your encouraging words, hugs and love. ♥ To my family; James, Raeisha, Christopher, Joshua, Seriah, Janisha and Kayla —thank you for supporting the vision with your prayers and love. ♥ ♥ A special thank you to the co-authors of the Occupy; **Prophetess Ayanna Lynnay, Dr. Lashonda Wofford, Dr. Shavona Whitehead, Dr. Tina Riley, Tyesha Cannon, Dr. Annette Watson-Johnson, Dr. Nancy V Brown , Dr. Helen Aguocha, Minister Danielle Hall and Dr. Latasha Stanley and Dr. Alisha Currie, PH.D**.

A special thank you my beautiful Jackie Hicks for her amazing photography, beautiful Letitia Thornhill for her gift of makeup artistry. Love you, ladies! ♥ To K.I.S.H. Home, Inc.'s board/advisors, volunteers and mentors; thank you for your dedication, support and believing in the vision of helping make a difference in the lives of young women in Delaware. To Emily Ann Warren, thank you for your support, love, and believing in me. To Prophetess Ayanna, publisher; I thank God every day for bringing you into my life. You have been a blessing. Thank you for your encouraging words, support, love and believing in the vision. Love you ♥ Lastly, but not least, I would like to thank D›vine Designs and everyone who encouraged, prayed for and supported K.I.S.H. Home, Inc. over the years, I am forever grateful. God Bless!

Meet
Dr. Kishma A. George

Dr. Kishma A. George, epitomizing the role of a "Dream Pusher," is a multifaceted professional, renowned for her inspirational speaking, entrepreneurial skills, and diverse creative roles. As an acclaimed prophetess, mentor, playwright, TV and radio personality, producer, and best-selling author, she dedicates herself to motivating individuals to realize their divine purpose. Her significant contributions include leading the Women Destined for Greatness Mentoring Program in Kent County, DE, focusing on empowering individuals regardless of their life's challenges.

As the President and CEO of K.I.S.H. Home, Inc. (Kingdom Investments in Single Hearts), Dr. George's vision is to positively impact the lives of girls and women in Delaware, particularly those transitioning from or aged out of the foster care system. Her experience as an Independent Living Mentor exposed her to the struggles faced by these young adults in achieving self-sufficiency and stability. Driven by a deep passion to assist, she established a 24-hour transitional home for young women, aiding their smooth transition to independent adulthood.

Dr. George's efforts have been widely recognized and celebrated in various media outlets, including the Dover Post, Delaware News Journal, Delaware State News, and Milford Beacon, as well as multiple magazines and radio shows. Her outstanding community involvement has earned her numerous awards, including Woman of the Year for Entrepreneurial Success, the Diversity Award from the State of Delaware, and the Authentic Servant Leadership Award.

At the core of her mission, Dr. George is committed to empowering others through the Word of God, inspiring them to pursue their dreams regardless of their circumstances. As the Director of the Women Destined for Greatness Mentoring Program and Visionary/Editor-in-Chief of K.I.S.H. Magazine, she continues to be a guiding force, ensuring that individuals realize and fulfill the dreams instilled within them by God.

Contact Information

Website: www.kishmageorge.com

Email: info@kishmageorge.com

Social Media

IG - @drkishmageorge

Facebook - Kishma George

TikTok- Kishma George

Linkedin - Kishma George

X- Kishma George

Blessed Assurance: Fulfilling My Destiny

By Dr. Tina L. Riley

The hymn *Blessed Assurance*, written by Fanny J. Crosby, beautifully encapsulates the profound joy and confidence of a believer who is anchored in Christ. The assurance of salvation and God's guidance grants the believer an unwavering sense of purpose. This blessed assurance is the foundation upon which I can build my life and fulfill the destiny God has set before me. It empowers me to pursue my purpose, overcome challenges, and live a life of service and faith.

The Power of Blessed Assurance

Life often presents challenges that test our faith, determination, and understanding of our purpose. In these moments, the assurance that *"I can do all things through Christ who strengthens me"* (Philippians 4:13) becomes a cornerstone of resilience and motivation. This scripture not only inspires hope but also provides a spiritual framework for overcoming obstacles and fulfilling my divine purpose. Embracing this truth helps me navigate life's challenges, align with God's plan rather than my own, and step confidently into my destiny.

The Source and Foundation of Assurance

Blessed assurance begins with an intimate relationship with God through Christ. This relationship is grounded in faith, as described in Hebrews 11:6: *"And without faith it is impossible to please God, because anyone who comes to him must believe that he exists and that he rewards those who earnestly seek him."* This assurance is not based on circumstances or personal achievements but on the unchanging nature of God and His promises.

The journey to fulfilling my destiny begins with understanding the foundation of my faith. According to Hebrews 11:1, *"Faith is the substance of things hoped for, the evidence of things not seen."* Through faith, I trust in Christ's power and promises. This trust allows me to view challenges not as insurmountable barriers but as opportunities for growth and spiritual development. Life provides countless opportunities to stretch my faith. When I affirm that I can do all things through Christ, I acknowledge that my strength is not my own but comes from a divine source—one that is limitless and eternal.

Faith in Action: David and Goliath

A powerful example of faith and assurance is seen in the story of **David and Goliath** (1 Samuel 17). David, a young shepherd, faced a giant warrior with nothing but a slingshot and stones. His confidence was not rooted in his own abilities but in his unwavering faith that God would deliver him. Likewise, by placing my faith in Christ, I can face the "giants" in my life with the blessed assurance that victory is possible through Him.

Overcoming Challenges and Self-Doubt with Assurance

Life is filled with obstacles that can make fulfilling my purpose seem daunting. However, blessed assurance provides the strength and resilience needed to overcome these challenges. Philippians 4:13 states, *"I can do all things through Christ who strengthens me."* This scripture reminds me that I am not alone in my journey and that Christ's power enables me to achieve what might seem impossible on my own.

Self-doubt is one of the greatest hindrances to fulfilling one's purpose. Negative self-perception and the fear of failure often lead to stagnation. However, the declaration of Philippians 4:13 counters these doubts by affirming that my capabilities are strengthened through Christ. This verse serves as a constant reminder of my potential and worth in God's eyes.

In moments of uncertainty, prayer and meditation on God's Word provide clarity and reassurance. Jeremiah 29:11 states, *"For I know the plans I have for you, declares the Lord, plans to prosper you and not to harm you, plans to give you hope and a future."* This promise reinforces that my life has divine purpose and that Christ's strength will guide me in fulfilling it. By internalizing these truths, I combat self-doubt and replace it with confidence in God's plan.

Living a Purposeful Life – Aligning with God's Purpose

Fulfilling my destiny requires intentionality and alignment with God's will. Proverbs 3:5-6 instructs, *"Trust in the Lord with all your heart and lean not on your own understanding; in all your ways submit to him, and he will make your paths straight."* By seeking God's guidance through prayer and Scripture, I can ensure that my decisions and actions align with His purpose for my life.

This alignment requires discernment, obedience, and surrender. Trusting in God allows me to release my own limited understanding and embrace His perfect wisdom. As I walk in faith, He directs my steps, ensuring that my pursuits are in harmony with His divine will.

Aligning with God's purpose also involves embracing a mindset of service. Jesus exemplified servant leadership, teaching that true greatness comes through serving others (Mark 10:43-45). By adopting this perspective, I recognize that my destiny is not solely about personal achievement but about making a meaningful impact on the lives of others. Through Christ's strength, I find the courage and resources to serve effectively, even in challenging circumstances.

Living a purposeful life means contributing to God's kingdom. Jesus modeled this in His ministry, teaching that **true greatness is found in serving others** (Mark 10:45). By cultivating a servant's heart, I not only fulfill my calling but also bring glory to God, reflecting His love through my actions.

Building Resilience Through Challenges

Life's challenges can feel overwhelming, but they also present opportunities for growth. James 1:2-4 encourages believers to *"consider it pure joy...whenever you face trials of many kinds, because you know that the testing of your faith produces perseverance."* By leaning on Christ, I develop resilience that equips me to face difficulties without losing sight of my purpose.

The Apostle Paul serves as a powerful example of perseverance. Despite enduring numerous hardships, including imprisonment and persecution, he remained steadfast in his mission, declaring, *"I have fought the good fight, I have finished the race, I have kept the faith"* (2 Timothy 4:7). Paul's unwavering reliance on Christ's strength enabled him to endure, and his testimony inspires me to press forward in faith, no matter the obstacles I encounter.

Practical Steps to Fulfill My Destiny

1. **Daily Communion with God** – Regular prayer and Bible study strengthen my relationship with Christ and provide spiritual nourishment.

2. **Setting God-Centered Goals** – Ensuring that my aspirations align with God's will helps me stay focused on my purpose.

3. **Surrounding Myself with a Supportive Community** – Fellow believers offer encouragement, accountability, and wisdom.

4. **Cultivating Gratitude** – A grateful heart fosters contentment and helps me recognize God's blessings in every situation.

5. **Taking Action in Faith** – Boldly stepping out in faith, even when the path is unclear, demonstrates trust in God's provision and guidance.

Living in Destiny

Blessed assurance is more than a comforting idea; it is the foundation upon which I build a life of faith, resilience, and purpose. Through the assurance of God's promises, I am empowered to overcome challenges, pursue my destiny, and live a life that reflects His glory.

As I trust in God's plan and rely on His strength, I am confident that I will fulfill the destiny He has prepared for me. The affirmation *"I can do all things through Christ who strengthens me"* is not just a statement—it is a lifestyle of faith, resilience, and purpose. By embracing this truth, I align with God's will and walk boldly in the path He has set before me.

With every step, I am reminded that this journey is not mine alone—it is a divine partnership with the One who holds my future securely in His hands. As I continue to trust in Christ's strength, I know that He is with me every step of the way, guiding, equipping, and empowering me to achieve His divine purpose for my life.

Meet
Dr. Tina L. Riley

Dr. Tina L. Riley is a distinguished leader and accomplished professional with a steadfast commitment to service, both in her career and her community. She currently serves as the Team Lead of the Support Branch and Security Programs Manager for the Department of Defense (DoD) at the Office of Prepublication and Security Review, located in the Pentagon, Washington, D.C. In this role, Dr. Riley oversees the comprehensive security program she established, ensuring the protection of personnel, information, and physical assets critical to the DoD and the Secretary of Defense.

Dr. Riley provides strategic oversight and management for the Support Branch, handling prepublication reviews, security clearances, and other vital processes related to the Office of the Secretary of Defense, Joint Staff, Military Services, Defense Agencies, Combatant Commands, and DoD Contractors. Her responsibilities include the development, implementation, and enforcement of security policies within her purview, reflecting her deep expertise and dedication to national security.

Beyond her professional achievements, Dr. Riley is a multifaceted individual with a passion for helping others. She is an Avon Ambassador, where her enthusiasm for beauty and self-care complements her entrepreneurial spirit. A devoted servant of God since childhood, Dr. Riley remains active in her faith, serving her community and offering support wherever needed. Known for her infectious laughter and love for people, she finds joy in uplifting others through her positive outlook and deep spirituality.

An Amazon #1 best-selling author, Dr. Riley has discovered a profound love for writing in recent years. She actively collaborates on various book projects, sharing her stories and testimonies to inspire and empower others. Her creative talents extend to crafting beautiful gift baskets for all occasions, a hobby that not only showcases her artistic abilities but also provides a relaxing and rewarding outlet. Creating baskets has become an entrepreneurial labor of love.

Dr. Riley's commitment to making a positive impact extends beyond her writing. She was invited to speak at a Juvenile Detention Center in Maryland, where her motivational speech for the Changing Habits and Making Positive Strides Program encouraged young people to make better choices for their futures. Looking ahead, she aspires to create a charity and transitional home for abused women, a vision she plans to pursue after her second retirement, with the guidance and blessings of God.

Originally from Ohio, Dr. Riley's early education was shaped by her time at a girl-centered Catholic school, where she developed a love for singing, performing in school chorus and gospel choirs. Although she is naturally bashful, her passion for music continues today as she sings with a local church's community choir and the Southern Maryland Regional Choir. A few years after high school graduation, she enlisted in the United States Air Force, where she served with distinction for 22 years before retiring as a disabled veteran.

Dr. Riley's academic credentials reflect her dedication to continuous learning and leadership development:

Education:

- 2005: Associate of Applied Science in Information Management, Community College of the Air Force

- 2007: Bachelor of Science in Occupational Education (Management), Wayland Baptist University

- 2010: Master's Certification in Project Management, Villanova University

- 2012: Honorary Doctorate of Humane Letters, Cornerstone Christian University

- 2014: Master of Science in Organizational Leadership, Argosy University

Dr. Tina L. Riley is a shining example of a life dedicated to service, leadership, and faith. She continues to inspire those around her through her unwavering commitment to excellence and her heartfelt desire to make a difference in the world.

Email: hello@tinariley.me

Website: https://tinariley.me

IG: hello@tinariley

FB: Tina Riley

Occupy the Broken Places

By Dr. LaTasha Stanley

Introduction:

My story begins in a place of pain I never deserved but endured nonetheless. As a child, I was molested. For years, I tried to bury this trauma in silence, believing that if I didn't speak about it, the weight would disappear. But silence doesn't erase wounds; it deepens them. The shame and confusion lingered, slowly eroding my sense of self. It left me questioning my worth and whether I would ever feel whole again.

Then came rejection. The people who should have embraced me most—those I thought I could trust—made me feel like an outsider. I was the "black sheep" of the family, the one who never quite measured up. Whether spoken aloud or communicated through actions, the message was clear: I wasn't enough. I felt as though I was always on the outside looking in, yearning for love and validation that never seemed to come. That rejection wasn't just external; it took root in my heart, convincing me that I wasn't worthy of love or belonging.

At just 14 years old, I became a mother. While other girls my age worried about school dances and passing notes in class, I worried about diapers. I held my baby in my arms, overwhelmed by love and responsibility. I didn't have a manual, a guide, or even consistent support to navigate motherhood. All I had was the determination that my child wouldn't feel the pain I had endured. But determination alone couldn't erase the challenges.

I was no longer just a child—I was a teenage mother in a world quick to dismiss me. People didn't see my heart; they only saw the situation. I was labeled, judged, and often ignored. But even as society tried to define me by my circumstances, I was quietly discovering my strength. Every hardship I faced became a brick in the foundation of resilience I didn't yet know I was building.

The rejection and pain I experienced were relentless. There were moments when I questioned if life would ever be more than struggle and survival. I felt like a failure, not just to others, but to myself. Yet, deep inside, there was a flicker of hope—small but steady. Even in my darkest moments, I refused to let the world's opinion of me be the final word.

I didn't know it then, but God was with me through it all. In the pain, He was present. In the rejection, He was whispering, "You are mine." Even when I found myself incarcerated and felt most abandoned, He was planting seeds of restoration. Behind those prison walls, where hope seemed distant, God's presence remained. Those seeds were invisible at the time, buried beneath layers of brokenness, regret, and doubt, but they were there.

It was in those moments of isolation that He began to remind me of who I was in Him—not the sum of my mistakes, but a work in progress, being molded for something greater. Looking back now, I see that every tear I cried, every hurt I endured, was part of a larger story. The pain didn't break me—it prepared me. The rejection didn't define me—it refined me. God wasn't just witnessing my suffering; He was using it to build something stronger, something greater than I could have ever imagined.

What others saw as the end of my story was only the beginning. Those early years of hardship weren't just my struggle—they became my testimony. They became proof of what God can do when you refuse to give up and when you trust Him to turn your pain into purpose.

Reclaiming My Identity

From a young age, I experienced rejection and trauma that left me questioning my worth and place in the world. I felt unseen, unloved, and disconnected from any sense of purpose. Being molested, feeling rejected, and becoming a mother at 14 were heavy burdens that could have crushed me completely. Yet, even in those dark moments, a small spark within me refused to go out—a whisper that there was more to life than the pain I was enduring.

As I navigated through these early struggles, I began to see God working in my life. Though I didn't fully understand it at the time, He was slowly revealing my value and purpose. One pivotal moment came when I realized that my circumstances didn't define me. I remember sitting alone one night, overwhelmed by the weight of my situation, and I cried out to God. It wasn't an eloquent prayer, but it was raw and honest: "Why me? What am I here for?"

That prayer would become even more significant when I found myself incarcerated. Being behind bars felt like hitting rock bottom, a place of complete isolation, where my mistakes and regrets surrounded me like walls I couldn't escape. At first, the shame was overwhelming. I wondered if this was all I was destined for, another chapter in a story of brokenness. But even in that space, God was present.

In those quiet moments of incarceration, I had no choice but to sit with myself and confront the life I had lived. It was painful, but it was also a turning point. God began to whisper to my spirit, "This is not the end of your story." He reminded me that even though I felt abandoned by the world, He had not abandoned me. He was using this time to strip away the lies I had believed about myself for so long.

I started to see that my mistakes and bad choices didn't disqualify me from God's grace. Instead, they were opportunities for Him to show His power to redeem and restore. During my time of incarceration, I began to rebuild from the inside out. I prayed, read Scripture, and reflected on how God could turn even the lowest point of my life into a foundation for something greater.

That season taught me that God can meet us in the places we least expect, even in a cell. He doesn't wait for us to be perfect or to have it all together. He comes to us in our brokenness, offering hope and a new beginning. My incarceration was not the end—it was a refining process. It was where I began to truly understand that my pain had a purpose, and my story could one day inspire others to overcome their own struggles.

That night, I felt a peace I had never known before, as if God Himself had wrapped His arms around me and whispered, "You are Mine." It was the beginning of a journey to discover my identity in Christ, a journey that wasn't easy, but one that was necessary.

I began to see my life through His eyes. I wasn't the "black sheep" that others labeled me—I was chosen. I wasn't just a teenage mother trying to survive—I was a vessel for His glory. Each moment of rejection, every tear shed, became part of a greater story He was writing.

Another turning point came when I began to study the Word of God more deeply. Scriptures like Psalm 139:14, *"I am fearfully and wonderfully made,"* and Jeremiah 29:11, *"For I know the plans I have for you,"* resonated deeply with me. These weren't just words on a page; they were promises. Promises that I was created with intention, that my pain had purpose, and that my identity was secure in Him.

God also used the people He placed in my life to affirm my worth. Mentors, friends, and even strangers spoke life into me when I couldn't see it for myself. Through their encouragement and His guidance, I began to let go of the lies I had believed about myself. I stopped defining myself by my past and started walking boldly in the truth of who I was becoming.

Reclaiming my identity didn't happen overnight. It was a process of unlearning and relearning. It required me to confront my fears, forgive those who hurt me, and trust that God had a plan even when I couldn't see it. But in every step, He was faithful.

Today, I stand as a woman who knows her worth—not because of what I've accomplished, but because of who God says I am. My identity is no longer rooted in the opinions of others or the mistakes of my past; it is firmly grounded in Christ.

I share this chapter of my journey to remind you that no matter what you've been through, your identity is not defined by your pain. You are chosen, loved, and created with purpose. God is always working, even in the midst of your struggles, to bring you into the fullness of who He has called you to be.

Embrace the journey.

Restoring Through Education

Mentoring and motivation became the bridge between who I was and who I was meant to be. It was my way of reclaiming power over my circumstances, breaking the limitations that life had placed on me, and stepping boldly into my God-given purpose.

For years, I carried the weight of rejection and trauma, but when I made the decision to pursue my education, I was no longer just surviving—I was restoring what had been taken from me.

Earning my Bachelor's in Business was the first major step in that journey. The idea of going back to school seemed almost impossible. But deep within me was a desire to not only provide for my family but to also break generational cycles of hardship. I wanted to show my children that education could open doors and create opportunities that no one could take away.

There were times when the challenges felt insurmountable—late nights studying, moments of doubt when I questioned if it was all worth it, and the constant battle to balance my responsibilities. But I pressed on, knowing that this journey was bigger than just earning a degree. It was about rewriting my story and creating a foundation for the future.

When I graduated with my Bachelor's in Business, I felt a sense of accomplishment that words cannot fully capture. It wasn't just a piece of paper; it was a symbol of resilience, determination, and faith. That degree represented every tear I had cried, every obstacle I had overcome, and every prayer I had prayed.

But God wasn't finished with me yet.

The decision to pursue my Doctorate in Theology was a leap of faith. By then, I had begun to understand that my life wasn't just about overcoming—it was about purpose. God had given me a testimony, and I knew I was called to share it. Earning my Doctorate was my way of equipping myself to not only walk in my calling but also empower others to do the same.

Studying theology was more than an academic pursuit—it was a spiritual awakening. Through every course, every lecture, and every late-night writing session, I gained a deeper understanding of God's Word and His plan for my life. It was in this season that I truly began to see how He had been working all along, even in my darkest moments.

Pursuing education wasn't just about personal growth—it was about restoration. It was about reclaiming the parts of myself that had been lost to pain, fear, and doubt. It was about proving to myself—and to the world—that I was more than my past.

Education gave me the tools to not only rebuild my life but to also pour into the lives of others.

Today, my degrees are not just accomplishments—they are testimonies. They are reminders of what can happen when you trust God, step out in faith, and refuse to let your circumstances define you. They are proof that restoration is possible, even for those of us who have walked through the fire.

If there's one message I want to leave with you, it's this: never underestimate the power of education to transform your life. Whether it's formal schooling, self-study, or learning through life's experiences, the pursuit of knowledge equips you to walk in your purpose with confidence and authority.

God used my journey through education to restore what had been broken, to give me a voice, and to prepare me for the work He had called me to do. And He can do the same for you.

Whatever your circumstances, know that it's never too late to learn, to grow, and to reclaim the power that lies within you.

Living Restored and Leading Others

My journey has been one of brokenness, healing, and restoration. From the pain of rejection and trauma to the challenges of early motherhood and the pursuit of education, I've learned that restoration is not about achieving perfection—it's about trusting God to turn every loss into gain. It's about allowing Him to take the shattered pieces of our lives and create something beautiful.

Restoration doesn't erase the pain or the scars; it transforms them into testimonies of God's faithfulness. Every trial I've endured has become a tool for helping others, a reminder that no matter how broken we may feel, God is capable of using our lives for His glory.

To those who feel stuck in their broken places, I want to encourage you: occupy them. Don't run from the pain or the challenges. Lean into them, because it is often in those very places that God does His greatest work. He is a God who specializes in restoration, in bringing beauty from ashes, and in turning mourning into joy.

Trust Him in the process. Restoration is not instant—it's a journey. There will be moments of doubt, fear, and even failure, but keep moving forward. Trust that God's plan for your life is greater than anything you can imagine. He is not just restoring what was lost; He is creating something new, something greater than what you thought you needed.

As I look back on my journey, I realize that every struggle prepared me to step into my purpose. I now have the privilege of leading others, showing them what is possible when you surrender to God's will and trust His timing. My life is not perfect, but it is full—full of His grace, His love, and His purpose.

If you take anything away from my story, let it be this: you are never too broken to be restored. You are never too far gone for God to use you. Every setback, every disappointment, every tear—He can use it all. Occupy your broken places. Stand firm in His promises. And when restoration comes—and it will—walk boldly in your purpose, knowing that He has equipped you for every good work.

God is faithful. Trust Him to write your story, because when He does, it will be a masterpiece.

Dr. Latasha's Acknowledgments

First and foremost, I give all glory and honor to God, the author and finisher of my faith, for taking my brokenness and using it to fulfill His divine purpose. Without His grace, this book would not exist.

To my family, especially my children, who have been my greatest blessings and constant motivation—thank you for loving me through every season. Your unwavering support and encouragement gave me the courage to share my story.

To my mentors and spiritual leaders who have guided me along this journey, thank you for seeing what I could not see in myself and for pouring into me with wisdom, prayer, and correction. Your influence has left an indelible mark on my life and ministry.

To my friends and faith community who stood with me in moments of brokenness, thank you for being God's hands and feet. Your words of encouragement, acts of kindness, and belief in me were lifelines in my darkest days.

To every person who has ever felt broken, rejected, or forgotten—this book is for you. My prayer is that these words remind you that God sees you, loves you, and has a plan to restore what was lost.

Finally, to the readers of *Occupy the Broken Places*—thank you for allowing me to walk this journey with you. I pray that you find healing, hope, and strength within these pages.

With deep gratitude,

Dr. Latasha Stanley

Meet
Dr. LaTasha Stanley

Dr. LaTasha Stanley is a resilient and inspiring woman whose life story is a testament to the power of faith, determination, and restoration. Overcoming a childhood marked by rejection and trauma, she became a mother at the age of 14. Despite the challenges of early motherhood and being labeled the "black sheep," she persevered, refusing to allow her circumstances to define her future.

With an unshakable commitment to breaking generational cycles of hardship, Dr. Stanley pursued higher education, earning a **Bachelor's degree in Business** and a **Doctorate in Theology**. Through her studies, she not only reclaimed her identity but also discovered her God-given purpose to lead and inspire others.

Today, Dr. Stanley is a proud mother of four grown children, a spiritual leader, and a passionate mentor. She uses her testimony to encourage others to trust God's restoration process and boldly walk in their purpose. Her journey from brokenness to restoration has equipped her to help others **occupy their broken places and transform their pain into power.**

Dr. Stanley is the founder of **She iMpAcTz Solutions** and **iMpAcTz Tax Pro Academy,** where she provides mentorship and training to aspiring entrepreneurs and tax professionals. Her vision is to empower others to achieve personal and professional success while staying rooted in faith and integrity.

When she's not leading, discipling, or mentoring, Dr. Stanley enjoys sharing motivational messages, studying Scripture, and spending quality time with her family. Her story is a living example that no matter how broken your past may seem, God can use it to build a brighter, more purposeful future.

Contact Information

Thank you for your encouragement, leadership, support and interest in my journey.

🌐 **Website:**https://www.sheimpactz.net

📧 **Email:**info@sheimpactz.net

📱 **Social Media:**

- Instagram: Dr. LaTasha Stanley

- Facebook: DrLatasha Stanley

- Twitter: @Sheimpactz2

- LinkedIn: Dr. LaTasha Stanley

Feel free to reach out for speaking engagements, mentorship opportunities, or to share how this book has impacted you.

Blessings,

Dr. Latasha Stanley

Standing Tall: Occupying Your God-Given Assignment

By: Dr. Lashonda Wofford

There is something profound about standing tall in a world that often tries to push you down. For me, standing tall didn't come naturally, nor did it come easily. It came through growth, struggles, pain, and ultimately, through maturing in God. I had to learn that standing tall was not merely about physical posture; it was about spiritual posture. It required me to anchor myself in the unshakable faith that God was not only my strength but also my purpose, my guide, and my destiny. To truly stand tall and occupy my God-given assignment, I had to undergo a transformation—one that matured me in ways I could never have imagined.

As I reflect on my journey, one phrase continually stands out: *"I had to mature in God in order to stand tall so that I could occupy my God-given assignment."* These words are etched deep within my soul because they capture the essence of my testimony. It wasn't just about growing in faith—it was about maturing, evolving, and becoming the woman God had called me to be.

Maturity in God requires more than attending church, reading scripture, or engaging in prayer. It is a deep, inward transformation that occurs when you fully surrender to God's will and trust Him, even when everything around you feels like it's falling apart.

For a long time, I struggled to stand firm in the midst of trials. Life would throw challenges my way, and I would feel shaken, uncertain, and often defeated. Then, I learned a vital lesson: *"I had to learn not to believe what my eyes saw or what my heart felt so that I could remain focused on God's end goal."* That was one of the hardest lessons of my life.

Faith Beyond Sight and Feelings

It's easy to be consumed by what you see and feel. As human beings, we rely heavily on our senses to interpret the world around us. But as I grew in my walk with God, I realized that faith calls us to rise above what we can physically see and emotionally feel. I had to train my spirit to trust in the unseen—to trust in the promises of God that had yet to manifest in my life.

There were countless times when my eyes saw only failure, disappointment, and setbacks. My heart felt the weight of grief, anger, and frustration. I had moments when I questioned whether I would ever make it through the storms. Yet, I came to understand that those moments were not meant to destroy me but to refine me. The crushing, the pressing, and the beatings all served a divine purpose. These trials were shaping me into the vessel God needed me to be in order to fully occupy the assignment He had ordained for my life.

The Crushing, Pressing, and Beatings

Ah, the crushing. No one likes to talk about it, but it is an inevitable part of the journey. The crushing is that moment when everything you thought you could rely on fails, and you are left with nothing but your faith. It is in those moments of crushing that God removes the impurities from your soul. The crushing strips away everything that is not like Him, everything that hinders you from standing tall. I experienced crushing on multiple levels—emotionally, spiritually, and even physically. The pain was often unbearable, but I now understand that it was necessary.

The pressing followed the crushing. It was as if God was using the weight of my circumstances to press out every ounce of doubt, fear, and insecurity from within me. The pressing was uncomfortable, and at times, I wanted to run from it. But I knew that if I allowed God to complete His work in me, I would come out stronger on the other side. The pressing prepared me for the responsibility of occupying my assignment. It taught me endurance, perseverance, and a deeper reliance on God's strength rather than my own.

Then came the beatings. These were the moments when I felt like life was hitting me from every direction—unexpected blows that left me feeling bruised and battered. Yet, even in the beatings, I found grace. God was using these experiences to toughen me up, to give me spiritual muscle so that I could withstand the attacks of the enemy. The beatings weren't meant to destroy me; they were meant to build me up.

I have many battle scars—some visible, others hidden deep within—but every scar tells a story. Every scar is a testimony of God's faithfulness and His ability to bring me through what seemed like impossible situations. And glory to God, I made it. Those scars serve as reminders that I have fought the good fight, and by His grace, I have overcome.

I did not fall.

I did not give up.

I stood tall, and I continue to stand tall, occupying the space that God has given me.

Occupying the Assignment

What does it mean to truly occupy your God-given assignment? It means stepping into the fullness of who God created you to be—without fear, without hesitation, and without apology. It means taking ownership of your calling, knowing that God has equipped you with everything you need to succeed. It means understanding that your life has divine purpose and that every trial, setback, and victory has prepared you for this moment.

To occupy your assignment, you must first recognize that it is a sacred task. It is not just about doing what you are good at; it's about doing what God has purposed you to do. For me, that meant overcoming self-doubt, fear, and the limitations others placed on me. It meant trusting that God had a plan for my life that was greater than anything I could have imagined.

I had to be willing to stand tall in the face of adversity, refuse to bow to the pressures of life, and keep my eyes fixed on God. Occupying my assignment required a level of faith that transcended the natural. It demanded boldness, courage, and an unwavering commitment to pursue the vision God placed within me. And as I matured in my walk with God, I realized that the assignment wasn't just for me—it was for those who would come after me, those who would be inspired by my testimony, and those who needed the encouragement to stand tall in their own God-given assignments.

Standing Tall in Victory

Today, I stand tall—not because of my own strength, but because of the strength of the One who called me. I stand tall because I have seen the faithfulness of God in my life. I stand tall because I have learned to trust Him even when I couldn't trace Him. I stand tall because I have matured in my faith and in my understanding of who I am in Christ.

The journey to occupying your God-given assignment is not easy. There will be crushing, pressing, and beatings along the way. But know this—every scar you bear is a testament to the battles you have fought and the victories you have won. Every moment of pain has a purpose, and every challenge you face is preparing you for the greater assignment that lies ahead.

So, to anyone reading this, I encourage you to stand tall. Trust that God has a plan for your life, and no matter what comes your way, He will equip you to occupy your assignment. Remember, the battle is not yours; it is the Lord's. And glory to God, you will make it—just as I did.

Practical Tips and Tools to Stand Tall and Occupy Your God-Given Assignment

1. Develop a Consistent Prayer Life

- **Tip:** Make prayer your first line of communication with God, not just when you're in trouble. Create a daily habit of talking to God and listening for His guidance.

- **Tool:** Set aside 10-15 minutes each day for quiet prayer time. Use a journal to record insights or directions you sense during your time with God.

2. Anchor Yourself in Scripture

- **Tip:** God's Word is your foundation. Regularly reading and meditating on scripture will help you stay focused on His promises, even in difficult times.

- **Tool:** Use Bible apps like YouVersion for daily reading plans or join a Bible study group for accountability. Start with scriptures that reinforce your identity and purpose, such as Jeremiah 29:11 or Ephesians 2:10.

3. **Guard Your Mind Against Doubt**

- **Tip:** Doubts will come, but don't let them take root. Capture negative thoughts and replace them with the truth of God's Word.

- **Tool:** Create a list of affirmations rooted in scripture. Repeat them when feelings of doubt, fear, or insecurity arise. Examples include "I am fearfully and wonderfully made" (Psalm 139:14) and "I can do all things through Christ who strengthens me" (Philippians 4:13).

4. **Surround Yourself with Supportive People**

- **Tip:** You don't have to go through life alone. Surround yourself with a community of believers who will pray for you, support you, and hold you accountable to your calling.

- **Tool:** Join a local or online Christian community, mentorship group, or Bible study. Reach out to trusted mentors or spiritual leaders who can encourage you in your God-given assignment.

5. **Build Spiritual Endurance**

- **Tip:** Just like physical endurance, spiritual endurance is built over time through trials. View challenges as opportunities to grow stronger in faith.

- **Tool:** When faced with difficulties, pause and ask, "What is God teaching me in this?" Keep a record of your growth and answered prayers to remind yourself of God's faithfulness.

6. **Walk by Faith, Not by Sight**

- **Tip:** Don't rely solely on what your eyes see or what your emotions feel. Trust that God is working behind the scenes, even when you can't see immediate results.

- **Tool:** Use a faith journal to document what you are believing God for. Write down His promises and any progress, no matter how small.

7. **Stay Focused on God's End Goal**

- **Tip:** Keep your eyes fixed on the bigger picture of what God is calling you to do. Don't let distractions or temporary setbacks derail your mission.

- **Tool:** Break down your God-given assignment into smaller, actionable steps. Set short-term and long-term goals aligned with your purpose and revisit them regularly.

8. **Embrace the Process**

- **Tip:** Crushing, pressing, and challenges are part of the process that prepares you for your assignment. Trust that God is refining you for greater purpose.

- **Tool:** Practice daily gratitude, even for difficult times. Keep a gratitude journal and list three things you're thankful for each day, focusing on how God is shaping you.

9. **Keep a Humble and Teachable Spirit**

- **Tip:** Growth requires humility. Remain open to learning, whether from God, scripture, mentors, or your experiences.

- **Tool:** Make a habit of asking God to reveal areas in your life where you need growth. Write down the lessons He teaches you and apply them.

10. **Declare Victory Over Your Assignment**

- **Tip:** Speak life into your calling. Declare that you will occupy the space God has ordained for you.

- **Tool:** Use daily declarations of faith. Write down powerful affirmations that align with your assignment and speak them out loud each morning, such as "I am called, equipped, and positioned by God to fulfill my purpose."

By incorporating these practical tips and tools into your daily routine, you will stand taller in your faith, mature in your relationship with God, and confidently occupy the God-given assignment He has set before you.

Dr. Lashonda's Acknowledgements

First and foremost, I give all glory and honor to God, whose grace and mercy have carried me through every challenge and trial. Without His divine guidance, I would not be standing tall today, fulfilling the assignment He has placed on my life. To God be the glory for every victory, lesson, and opportunity to serve.

To my incredible family—especially my loving husband, Travis, my children, and my grandchildren—thank you for your constant love, support, and prayers. Your encouragement has been my anchor, and your belief in me has kept me pressing forward, even in the most difficult times. I love you all deeply.

To my parents, George and Beverly, my sister, Dawanna, and all those who have walked with me on this journey, your unwavering support and understanding have been a source of strength. I am grateful for the moments when you lifted me up when I felt weak and reminded me of my purpose.

To the *All Bets On Me* community and every woman who has stood with me on this journey, thank you for allowing me the privilege to speak into your lives. Your stories of resilience inspire me daily, and I am blessed to walk alongside you as we pursue our God-given assignments together.

Finally, to my Marketplace Mentor, Dr. Frances Ann Bailey, **my** Biz Bestie, Dr. Catherine Latoya Grant-Alston**,** and every person who has ever spoken a word of encouragement, prayed for me, or believed in the vision God gave me—thank you. You played a crucial role in helping me stand tall. May God bless you abundantly as you continue to walk in your own purpose and assignment.

Together, we stand tall in Christ, knowing that He is faithful to complete the good work He has started in us.

Meet
Dr. Lashonda Wofford

Dr. Lashonda Wofford is a dynamic entrepreneur, community advocate, and transformational leader. As the founder and driving force behind multiple successful ventures—including an affirmation collection, L&S Consulting Group, and Wofford & Williams Inc. DBA Akins Helping Hands, a thriving seven-figure home care company based in North Carolina—Dr. Wofford has established herself as a powerful force in both business and personal development. Now adding the title of freelance writer to her accomplishments, she continues to expand her impact.

Passionate about empowering others, Dr. Wofford created the **"All Bets on Me"** platform on Facebook, where she inspires individuals to invest in themselves and overcome life's challenges. Her journey, marked by resilience and determination, has led her to achieve numerous goals despite significant adversities. With a PhD in Christian Education, she stands as a beacon of success, particularly for women of color, breaking barriers and paving the way for others to access the same opportunities she has created.

Dr. Wofford's achievements are numerous and impactful. She is an accredited certified instructor and Founder of The All Bets On Me Academy, in partnership with Purpose Zeal Academy. She holds certifications as an executive leadership coach, life recovery coach, mental health counselor, and transformational coach—just to name a few.

A prolific author, she is an international nine-time best-selling author, with titles including:

- *Blessed Not Broken, Vol. I*

- *Igniting Your Purpose*

- *90 Days of Biblical Affirmations for Christian Women in Business and Ministry*

- *Love Business Marriage*

- *Marketplace Mogul*

- *Girl, Let That Go*

- *Pain Equals Purpose* (her solo work)

- Visionary of *Breaking the Chains: Liberating Your Lineage from Generational Curses*

Her contributions to literature and community service have earned her numerous accolades, including:

- 2022 ACHI Award for Public Service

- 2023 Author of the Year (InspireU Network)

- 2023 Coach of the Year (The Power and Grace Leadership Association)

- Recipient of Two Presidential Lifetime Achievement Awards

- Nationwide Registries Women of Distinction 2024 Honors Edition

- 2024 International Impact Book Award (*Pain Equals Purpose* - Autobiography, Female Empowerment, and Inspirational categories)

- 2024 Author of Influence (DWAP - Designed with a Purpose)

- 2024 Visionary Author of the Year (Global Iconic Changemakers of the 21st Century Award, BPMI Ladies Clubs Global Teas & Birthing Process Ministries International, United States of America)

Deeply rooted in her faith, Dr. Wofford and her husband are active members of Mt. Zion AME Zion Church, where she strives to live out God's plan for her life by serving others.

In her personal life, she cherishes time with her family, especially her grandchildren, and prioritizes self-care through relaxation and reading. Residing in **North Carolina** with her husband and family, Dr. Wofford continues to inspire and lead by example.

Connect with Dr. Lashonda Wofford:

- Website: www.drlashondawofford.com

- Facebook: [facebook.com/lashonda.
wofford.72mibextid=LQQJ4d] (https://www.facebook.com/
lashonda.wofford.72mibextid=LQQJ4d)

- All Bets On Me: [facebook.com/groups/1124117394775943/]
(ttps://www.facebook.com/groups/1124117394775943/)

- All Things Coaching Community:

[facebook.com/groups/1097641824230355/] (https://www.
facebook.com/groups/1097641824230355/)

All Bets On Me:
https://dr-lashonda-wofford-s-school.teachable.com/p/abom

Escape

By Dr. Alisha Currie

It all started on April 29, 1982, on a spring Thursday afternoon. A storm seemed to be coming—hard winds blew through the air, accompanied by a light rain. After thoughts of being aborted and hours of labor, a precious little girl soldier was born. As she entered this world crying, unfamiliar with her new surroundings, she had no idea that the storm she was born into would later become the storm she would have to endure.

For a while, the newly titled mother seemed happy with her newborn baby girl. This was her firstborn, and even though the little girl's father wasn't around, the mother vowed always to be there for her.

As the years passed, the little girl began to notice that her mother was rarely around. There were moments when she would stretch out her arms, hoping for a hug, only to come up empty, grasping nothing but air and space. Her mother was too busy embracing the streets—clubbing, drinking, and chasing a different life. Unfortunately, this left a hole in the little girl's heart. She couldn't understand why her mother was barely there.

The year was now 1987, and at just five years old, she still couldn't comprehend why her mother was absent so often. Her grandmother, witnessing the hurt her granddaughter carried, stepped in to fill that void. While enduring her own struggles, her grandmother became the steady presence the little girl desperately needed. But even with her grandmother's love, the shadows of her circumstances loomed over her. Nightmares began to form— nightmares born from real-life events that deeply scarred her young mind.

Her mother eventually found love and got married. At nine years old, the young girl faced a bittersweet moment—she had to leave her grandmother's home to move in with her mother and stepfather. She was excited to have a father figure but heartbroken to leave the woman who had been her safe haven for so many years. Her mother, understanding their bond, allowed her to finish the school year with her grandmother. Even so, the thought of moving weighed heavily on the young girl, affecting her focus in school.

As a result, she had to repeat the fourth grade—a devastating blow to her confidence. She couldn't shake the words her grandfather had spoken about her in the past, and she felt like a failure. Imagine being a ten-year-old girl spending an entire summer knowing she would have to repeat a grade she had just completed. The only silver lining was that her new school would be in a different place, where no one would know her past.

Spending that summer with her grandmother helped block out the negativity. Her grandmother's house was more than a home; it was her sanctuary. It held some of the happiest memories— family gatherings, holidays with her aunts, cousins, and close friends. Whenever she thought of happiness, she envisioned her grandmother's house.

But one particular day stood out like a sore thumb. She had gone to the grocery store with one of her favorite aunts. While there, they ran into a store worker who knew her aunt. As the conversation carried on, the worker turned to the young girl and then back to her aunt, asking, *"Who is this dark-skinned girl with you?"*

The question hit her like a punch. Instantly, she thought back to all the negative things her grandfather had said about her appearance. Though her aunt laughed it off, hoping her niece hadn't fully registered the comment, the damage was already done. A deep sadness settled in.

The ride home was silent. She sat in quiet reflection, wondering, *Why don't I look like everyone else in my family? Why am I the dark one?* The young girl began to hate herself. Depression started to take root.

So many thoughts ran through her mind—starting at a new school, wondering if she would make friends, and holding on to every negative word spoken about her. She didn't know how to escape these feelings at such a young age. She considered telling her mother but quickly dismissed the thought, thinking, *She's just going to brush me off.*

So, she decided to stay silent.

The first day of the school year arrived, and despite her inner battles, she was happy to be in a home with her mother and stepfather. Finally, she had someone she could call "Dad," someone who would love her like a father should. Slowly, her feelings of sadness began to fade.

A few weeks into the new school year, she realized that repeating the fourth grade wasn't so bad after all. She made new friends, and no one knew about her past struggles. She was in a good place. Her stepfather even came to her school to check on her when her mother couldn't. He attended all her school programs, making her feel seen and valued.

For the first time in a long time, she felt like she was escaping the trauma.

Meet
Alisha Currie

I am, first and foremost, a child of the Lord. Secondly, I am a wife, mother, sister, and friend.

I released my first book, *Prisoner of the Mess*, and I serve as the First Lady and Co-Pastor of Currie The Cross Church. My motivation and constant passion is Jesus! The Lord has blessed me to be a business owner alongside my husband, and together, we seek Him for direction in every step we take.

There is a joy within me that I simply cannot keep to myself. As I continue to listen to the Lord, I am committed to walking boldly in my purpose.

Contact Information

Facebook : Alisha Currie

Instagram: firstladyalishacurrie

TikTok: @firstladycurrie

Email adress: curriealisha2014@gmail.com

Alisha's Dedication:

I dedicate this chapter to my beloved grandmother, **Leola Paige**, who now rests in Heaven. Your love and legacy continue to inspire me.

To my faithful and God-fearing husband, **Dr. Marlowe Currie**— you are my rock, my covering, and my greatest blessing. I love you deeply.

And last but certainly not least, to my beautiful children—I love you more than words can express. You are my heart and my joy.

Occupy: Rise and Reclaim Your Purpose

By Dr. Nancy V. Brown Willis

Introduction: Occupying Your God-Given Destiny

Life may come with unexpected pain and detours, but no matter the trauma, there is hope. Occupy is a call to rise, take action, and reclaim the dreams, purpose, and destiny God intended for you. Despite life's challenges, you can walk in healing, rebuild your confidence, and restore your relationship with God.

My journey has been filled with seasons of heartbreak, rejection, and doubt. I know what it feels like to question whether joy and purpose are still possible. Yet, I also know what it feels like to stand back up, occupy the space God created for me, and live a life of impact and peace.

Through this chapter, I'll share personal insights and practical steps to help you navigate from pain to purpose.

1. Embrace the Power of Healing

The first step to occupying your dreams is healing from the wounds that hold you back. Trauma may try to paralyze you, but healing is a journey you can choose to take.

Practical Tips for Healing:

- Acknowledge Your Pain: Healing begins with honesty. God already knows your heart; you don't have to hide your emotions from Him. Journaling your thoughts is a powerful way to release pain.

- Forgiveness as Freedom: Forgiveness isn't about excusing what happened but releasing its grip on your life. Pray for the strength to forgive, and ask God to help you let go of bitterness.

- Seek Support: Healing is not meant to be done in isolation. Find a trusted counselor, mentor, or faith-based recovery group to walk alongside you.

Personal Reflection: I had to face my wounds head-on and seek both God and wise counsel. Only then did I truly step into my calling.

2. Rebuild Self-Confidence Through God's Eyes

Trauma often shatters our sense of worth, making us feel unworthy or incapable of success. Rebuilding self-confidence is not about arrogance; it's about seeing yourself as God sees you—fearfully and wonderfully made.

Practical Tips for Rebuilding Confidence:

- Speak Life Over Yourself: Replace negative self-talk with affirmations rooted in God's Word. Say, "I am chosen. I am loved. I am capable."

- Celebrate Small Wins: Growth is a process. Acknowledge every step forward, no matter how small.

- Step Out Despite Fear: Confidence grows with action. When you take small, courageous steps, you begin to trust yourself again.

Personal Reflection: I learned that confidence was not about perfection but about trusting God in the process.

3. Reconnect with God: The Key to Occupying Your Purpose

Walking in your destiny requires a strong, intentional relationship with God. He is the author of your purpose and the healer of your heart.

Practical Tips for Rebuilding Your Relationship with God:

- Daily Connection: Spend time in prayer, worship, and reading Scripture. These moments strengthen your foundation.

- Be Honest in Prayer: God desires a real relationship, not a performance. Pour out your heart to Him without filters.

- Practice Gratitude: Gratitude shifts your perspective and reminds you of God's faithfulness, even in hard seasons.

Personal Reflection: There were times I didn't feel worthy to come before God, but He reminded me that His love never wavers.

4. Occupy: Walk Boldly into Your Purpose

The final step is action. You can't simply wish for healing and purpose—you must step into it. God has already equipped you with everything you need.

Practical Tips for Occupying Your Destiny:

- Use What's In Your Hand: Start with what you have. You don't need perfection or resources to begin.

- Be Faithful with the Small Things: God honors consistency. When you steward what you have, He multiplies it.

- Stay in Purpose, Not Comparison: Your journey is unique. Don't be distracted by someone else's path.

Personal Reflection: When I focused on what God placed in my hands rather than what I lacked, doors began to open.

Conclusion: Occupy and Thrive

No matter what you've been through, you can rise, heal, and occupy your destiny. You are not defined by your trauma but by the God who redeems and restores.

5. Prioritizing Self-Care and Self-Love: Guarding Your Heart and Growth

To fully occupy your purpose, you must learn to care for yourself holistically—spiritually, mentally, emotionally, and physically. Self-care and self-love are not selfish; they are essential for sustaining the energy, clarity, and strength needed to walk in destiny.

Equally important is guarding your environment. Not everyone will support your growth. Some people will try to trap you with negativity, manipulation, or jealousy. Recognizing these unhealthy relationships and creating boundaries is an act of self-love.

Practical Tips for Practicing Self-Care and Self-Love:

- Create Sacred Spaces: Dedicate time for activities that replenish your spirit, such as prayer, nature walks, journaling, or creative expression.

- Nourish Your Body: Eat well, rest intentionally, and move your body in joyful ways. Your physical health directly impacts your mental clarity and emotional resilience.

- Speak Kindly to Yourself: Replace self-criticism with words of love and encouragement. Ask yourself, Would I say this to a friend?

Guarding Your Environment:

- Discern Energy Drainers: Pay attention to how people make you feel. Those who belittle your dreams or sow seeds of doubt may not belong in your inner circle.

- Establish Boundaries: It's okay to say "no" to situations and relationships that compromise your peace and growth. Boundaries protect your heart and purpose.

- Surround Yourself with Growth-Minded People: Seek out those who challenge and uplift you spiritually and mentally.

Biblical Reminder: "Above all else, guard your heart, for everything you do flows from it." — Proverbs 4:23

Personal Reflection

I had to learn that not everyone who smiled in my face genuinely wanted to see me succeed. Some were simply spectators, waiting for me to fail. Others were actively working against me, masked in false support. It was a hard lesson, but a necessary one. Letting go of relationships filled with negativity and manipulation freed me to focus on my healing and growth. It was only when I walked away from those toxic connections that I saw the doors God had been waiting to open for me.

When I made room by releasing what no longer served me, God blessed me with new relationships that aligned with my destiny— people who prayed for me, encouraged me, and genuinely wanted to see me thrive. I realized that occupying my purpose wasn't just about what I was called to do; it was also about who I surrounded myself with.

Your environment matters.

Occupying your purpose starts with the love you give yourself and the atmosphere you cultivate around you. When you prioritize your well-being—spiritually, mentally, and emotionally—and align yourself with God's truth about who you are, you step boldly into destiny. You walk forward, unshaken by the traps others might set beneath your feet, confident that God has already prepared a path for you.

Let go of anything or anyone that keeps you from fully occupying the space God has designed for you. Make room for His divine connections, His direction, and His promises. Your purpose is too great to be hindered by those who were never meant to walk with you in the first place.

6. Breaking Free from the Shackles of Silence and Shame

Silence and shame are powerful chains that can keep us trapped in pain and isolation. When we carry the weight of unspoken trauma, it festers, leading to feelings of worthlessness, loneliness, and hopelessness. But there is healing in speaking your truth and telling your story.

I am a suicide survivor and have also lost my sister to suicide. We both needed someone like us to help us survive—someone who understood our pain and could offer hope. For too long, I lived in silence, believing that my pain had to remain hidden. But I learned that sharing my truth not only set me free but also gave others permission to seek help and find healing.

Your story holds the power to save lives.

Steps to Break Free and Speak Your Truth

- **Acknowledge the Power of Your Voice** – Silence only strengthens shame. When you speak, you take back your power.

- **Start Small** – You don't have to share everything all at once. Begin by writing your thoughts in a journal or talking to someone you trust.

- **Remember You Are Not Alone** – Many have walked similar paths. By sharing your story, you become a beacon of hope for them.

- **Seek Professional Support if Needed** – Speaking your truth may bring up painful memories. Counselors and support groups can guide you through this process safely.

- **Focus on Impact, Not Judgment** – Your story will touch hearts, even if some people don't understand. You are speaking for those who need to hear your truth.

Why Sharing Your Story Saves Lives

1. **It Normalizes the Conversation Around Mental Health** – Many people feel alone in their struggles. Hearing your story reminds them they are not isolated.

2. **It Encourages Others to Seek Help** – When someone hears how you found healing, it gives them the courage to reach out too.

3. **It Breaks Generational Chains** – By addressing trauma openly, you create a legacy of transparency and healing for future generations.

Personal Reflection

Speaking openly about my own survival and loss has connected me with countless people who needed to hear they weren't alone. If my voice can save just one life, it's worth it.

You are not defined by your trauma or your silence. There is courage inside of you waiting to be unleashed. Speak your truth—someone is waiting to hear your story. Your voice has the power to change and even save lives.

Shame Is a Trick of the Enemy

Shame is one of the enemy's greatest weapons, designed to keep you in bondage and silence. It whispers lies that you are unworthy, broken, and beyond redemption. But God says otherwise—He calls you loved, forgiven, and whole.

The enemy knows that when you step out of shame and into truth, you break free from his grip. Speaking your truth dismantles the power of shame and exposes it for the lie that it is. Remember, shame loses its power when you bring it into the light.

God has given you the strength to overcome. Do not let the enemy keep you captive—your voice is your victory.

Occupy your life. Occupy your healing. Occupy your purpose. The world needs the greatness that's inside you.

Dr. Nancy's Acknowledgments

First and foremost, I give honor and glory to God for His grace, guidance, and unfailing love throughout every step of my journey. Without His presence, I would not be where I am today.

To my incredible husband, thank you for your unwavering love, strength, and support. Your belief in me has been a constant source of encouragement.

To my beloved mother, your wisdom, resilience, and prayers have shaped who I am. I am forever grateful for your example of strength and unconditional love.

To my amazing children—Deisha, Kevon, Malik, and Christian— you are my pride and joy. Watching you grow and walk in your own journeys inspires me every day.

To my beautiful grandchildren, thank you for bringing joy and light into my life. Your smiles remind me of the beauty and hope in each new day.

To my extended family, friends, and all those who have supported me along the way, I am deeply grateful for your love and encouragement.

This journey would not have been possible without each of you. Thank you for standing with me as I continue to walk in purpose and share my story to help others heal, grow, and thrive.

Meet
Dr. Nancy V. Brown Willis

Makeup & Photography by: Joanna Petit-Frere

Dr. Nancy V. Brown Willis is a Christian counselor, corporate chaplain, holistic life coach and consultant dedicated to helping individuals heal from trauma, overcome addictions, and cultivate self-love. As an advocate for suicide prevention and child sexual abuse (CSA) recovery, Dr. Nancy is passionate about empowering others to rediscover hope, rebuild self-confidence, and walk boldly into their God-given purpose.

A native of Costa Rica, Dr. Nancy blends faith-based principles with practical strategies to guide individuals on their journey to wholeness. Through her coaching programs, speaking engagements, and written works, she provides transformative tools for healing and personal growth.

A devoted wife, mother, and grandmother, Dr. Nancy finds joy in spending time with her family and inspiring others to rise above adversity and thrive in faith, purpose, and destiny.

Contact Dr. Nancy:

Website: www.nancyvbrown.com

Email: Nancyvbrown100@gmail.com

Instagram: nancyvbrown & nancyvbrownministries

Facebook: drnancyvbrown & nancyvbrownministries

IG/FB Youth Coaching: bravegirlsriseup

The Realm of Possibility

By Danielle N. Hall

A word I often find myself using is capacity. According to the *Cambridge Dictionary*, capacity is defined as "someone's ability to do a particular thing." *Collins Dictionary* offers several synonymous terms, including ability, power, strength, size, room, and range.

There have been many times in my life when I felt as though I was at full capacity—no room on my plate to add even a morsel, let alone a crumb, and no strength to carry what I perceived as a burden. When new projects, assignments, or thoughts presented themselves, it was overwhelming and would trigger an anxious, fearful response. My heart rate would increase, my palms would grow sweaty, and my right leg would begin to shake rapidly. Another response, which was unorthodox to say the least, was that I would start humming a popular (but completely unrelated) tune: *"Here Comes the Bride."* Judge me not—I have the same question that you do about why that particular song would come to mind. I digress.

The matter at hand is how the presentation of something new or more would invoke a negative response. As a Believer, I still experienced this initial reaction, but over time, it became shorter-lived. I have learned to truly encourage myself in the Lord and with His Word. Rather than focusing on my perceived limited capacity, I remind myself that *I can do all things through Christ who strengthens me* (Philippians 4:13). I love the Amplified version:

I can do all things [which He has called me to do] through Him who strengthens and empowers me [to fulfill His purpose—I am self-sufficient in Christ's sufficiency; I am ready for anything and equal to anything through Him who infuses me with inner strength and confident peace].

What once seemed impossible or unworkable becomes possible. My mindset stretches, and as a result, my capacity to do all things that He has called me to becomes a reality. I now dwell in a place I love to call "The Realm of Possibility."

For every behavior, there is a root cause. Sometimes, we operate out of fear. Fear, in and of itself, is a natural response. We are wired to survive, so when faced with a perceived threat or danger, the fight-or-flight response is activated. The problem arises when fear becomes excessive.

I recall being a little girl when my late mother, whom I affectionately called Pearl, took me to a nearby playground. She wanted me to jump over the wooden border surrounding the small play area. It truly wasn't that high, but my mind perceived the obstacle as much larger than it was. I was terrified. Nevertheless, I eventually decided to give it a try.

At first, my thoughts were clouded with worst-case scenarios: *This wood is going to trip me. I could fall flat on my face. I could knock a tooth loose!* But then, something shifted in my mind. I finally decided that even if I fell, at least I had jumped—and I could always get back up.

The more my mind opened to the possibility of success, the smaller my fear became. And guess what? I did it! I took the jump, and I did NOT fall. The next jump became easier, and eventually, the fear disappeared completely.

But why was I so afraid to take the jump in the first place?

I have an idea.

I grew up in a nuclear household where my late father was unquestionably the most dominant presence in our home. With a military background, he ran a tight ship. Though I wasn't a child who made much noise or caused trouble, he was extremely strict.

I vividly remember having a cold once and struggling with a persistent cough. We were riding in the car, and I was in the backseat when he suddenly told me to stop coughing so much. It seemed so insensitive—even absurd. Naturally, I was afraid to cough after his command. It was uncomfortable, but I held it in.

To be clear, my father was a sacrificial and thoughtful man, but he was equally intimidating. He was a no-nonsense guy, and I was afraid of disappointing or upsetting him.

My father was also very protective. Some of his concerns were valid—he had a prophetic anointing and foresaw impending dangers. But some of his concerns were not revealed by God; they simply stemmed from his own worries as a father. This caused me to live a sheltered childhood where fear and anxiety were often present.

I became introverted, afraid of unfamiliar and new experiences. The cap on my capacity was firmly in place.

When I became an adult, I was still introverted but decided to open up—just a little—beyond my comfort zone.

Part of this was driven by motherhood. At 21, I became a mom, and suddenly, I wasn't just responsible for myself—I was responsible for a child who couldn't fend for herself.

When she was still a newborn, I found my way to the church where I received salvation and was baptized. It was at this church that I met someone I call Sisfrienmen, a woman who became the catalyst for my spiritual growth. She led the music ministry with both wisdom and example, showing me what a life fully submitted to Christ looked like.

By the time I encountered Sisfrienmen, I had already been married and had two sons. My late husband, who was nine years my senior, was used to me being a homebody—focusing solely on him, the children, and the home. But when I sat under Sisfrienmen's leadership, I began to fully submit to the Lord.

This meant doing what was uncomfortable. It required more of me.

My husband did not like this new version of me. He frequently threatened divorce, and at times, the little girl inside me—the one who feared disappointing her father—began to resurface.

But something had changed. This time, I chose faith over fear.

I studied the Word. I listened to worship music. I filled my spirit with God's truth. The capacity cap began to loosen.

The fear of opposition, rejection, and discomfort began to fade away.

As my spiritual journey continued, Romans 8:28 became my anchor:

And we know that all things work together for good to them that love God, to them who are the called according to His purpose.

I truly began to believe that everything—the good, the bad, the unexpected—was working together for God's greater plan. The more I focused on Him, the greater my capacity grew.

In June 2011, I both received and answered my call into ministry. I won't lie—I was nervous. Ministry carried great responsibility, and I didn't know what to expect. But the more God led me, the more I trusted Him.

I began sharing daily nuggets of wisdom on social media, which later became my first published book, *Dew Drops: Refreshing for the Soul.*

That was just the beginning.

My pen stayed active. I started a blog, *Danielle's Place*, to share real-life experiences and offer hope to others.

One of my most well-received blog posts, "Dirty Little Secrets and the Little White Lie," led to my second book—a poetic acknowledgment of my experiences as a survivor of childhood sexual abuse.

From there, the V.O.I.C.E. Ministry was born (Victorious Overcomers Inspiring Christian Empowerment), empowering women to heal from trauma through Christ's truth.

Fast-forward to today, and I stand in a space I never imagined occupying.

The once timid, introverted girl is now a minister, author, entrepreneur, and counselor—all because I said, "Yes, Lord."

And today, I walk forward, knowing that with every assignment He gives me, He will equip me.

With inner strength and confident peace, I step boldly into my rightful place to fulfill my destiny.

Danielle's Acknowledgements

I would like to acknowledge **my Lord and Savior** for giving me the courage and ability to complete my God-given assignments. Without His strength and guidance, none of this would be possible.

I also want to express my heartfelt gratitude for my **late parents**, who demonstrated what a life poured out in service and love truly looks like. Their example continues to inspire me.

Special thanks to everyone who has poured into my spiritual life, encouraging, teaching, and guiding me along this journey. Your impact has been invaluable, and I am forever grateful.

Meet
Danielle N. Hall

Danielle N. Hall is a Board-Certified Christian Counselor and Mental Health Coach, passionate about helping others recognize and achieve their divine purpose. In addition to her counseling work, she is a licensed minister, continually seeking ways to enlighten, encourage, and empower others through life's journey.

A sexual abuse overcomer, Danielle is the visionary and founder of **V.O.I.C.E.** (*Victorious Overcomers Inspiring Christian Empowerment*), a ministry dedicated to serving women who have experienced sexual assault or abuse.

She is the sole author of three books:

- *Dew Drops: Refreshing for the Soul* (her debut book)

- *Dirty Little Secrets & The Little White Lie* (Amazon #1 Bestseller)

- *Grace to Endure: You Don't Know My Story*

Additionally, she has contributed to **five book collaborations**:

- *She Wouldn't Let Me Fall* (2018)

- *Hope for the Overcomer's Soul* (2018)

- *My Whole Self Matters: Empowerment Journey Journal* (2019)

- *My Praise Is My Weapon* (2020)

- *God Blocked It* (2023)

In 2023, she also presented her first book collaboration, *The Heart That Forgives.*

Beyond her writing, Danielle is a budding entrepreneur. She is the owner of:

- **SOL by Danielle**, a greeting card service launched in 2017.

- **The Butterfly Effect by Danielle**, a butterfly-themed jewelry company launched in August 2019.

- **The R.O.P.E., LLC (The Realm of Possibility Experience)**, launched in May 2023, where she employs her expertise as a coach and counselor.

A recently widowed mother of three, Danielle is committed to achieving and maintaining balance amidst the demands of family, work, ministry, and personal growth.

Contact Information:

Danielle N. Hall
Email - mrsdaniellehall@yahoo.com
FB - Author, Danielle N. Hall
IG - thebutterflyeffect_bydanielle
Website: www.THEROPELLC.
com & www.thebutterflyeffectbydanielle.com

Embracing Destiny: Rising from Fear to Ulfillment

By Dr. Shavona L. Whitehead

For a long time, I lived in the shadows of my own potential. I felt the pull of purpose deep in my spirit, but fear kept me bound. It wasn't the kind of fear that shouted loudly—it whispered, quietly convincing me that I wasn't enough.

I heard God calling me to more. He whispered through sermons, scriptures, and even conversations with others. I felt the weight of His words pressing on my heart, but I pushed them aside. Instead of stepping forward, I stepped back. I was paralyzed—not by the challenges ahead, but by the doubts I held within.

"Why me?" I'd ask. *"Surely, someone else is better suited for this."* I didn't think I was strong enough, capable enough, or worthy enough. I lived in an uneasy truce between who I was and who God was calling me to be.

But God didn't give up on me. His call never quieted, and His love never stopped pursuing me.

The Weight of Shrinking Back

The truth is, fear doesn't just stop you—it shapes you. The more I hesitated to step into my calling, the smaller I felt. I became the woman who played it safe, staying within the comfort of what I thought I could manage.

The Bible tells the story of the Israelites standing at the edge of the Promised Land, too afraid to enter because of the giants they saw (Numbers 13:31-33). I understood their hesitation deeply. Like them, I saw only the obstacles and forgot the **God who had promised victory**.

It wasn't that I doubted God's power—I doubted that His power could work **through me**. I had made fear my companion and insecurity my constant counselor.

But then came a moment that changed everything.

A Command to Rise

One evening, during a quiet prayer, I heard a whisper in my heart so clear it silenced my doubts: *"I have chosen you. Do not be afraid. Occupy the land I have given you."*

The words felt heavy, not with burden but with promise. I realized then that shrinking back wasn't humility—it was disobedience. God wasn't asking me to rely on my strength; He was asking me to trust His.

I thought of Joshua, standing on the threshold of leading a nation into the Promised Land. God's words to him echoed in my spirit: *"Be strong and courageous. Do not be afraid; do not be discouraged, for the Lord your God will be with you wherever you go"* (Joshua 1:9).

God was asking me to trust Him the same way. To stop looking at what I lacked and start focusing on His sufficiency.

The Battle Within

The hardest part of stepping into purpose isn't the challenges outside—it's the ones within. I had to confront the lies I had believed for so long:

- *You're not good enough.*

- *You'll fail.*

- *Who do you think you are to take up this space?*

Those lies had become a fortress around my heart. But God's Word became the weapon I used to tear them down.

I started speaking truth over myself:

- *"I am fearfully and wonderfully made"* (Psalm 139:14).

- *"I can do all things through Christ who strengthens me"* (Philippians 4:13).

- *"God has not given me a spirit of fear, but of power, love, and a sound mind"* (2 Timothy 1:7).

It wasn't an overnight transformation. Every step forward felt like a battle. But with each victory, I began to see myself the way God sees me—not as someone defined by my past or my flaws, but as someone called and equipped for His purpose.

Walking in Dominion

As I grew in faith, I began to understand what it truly meant to occupy the promise. God wasn't asking me to passively wait for His blessings—He was asking me to step into them with authority.

Walking in dominion means recognizing the authority God has given you. Luke 10:19 became a foundational scripture for me:

"I have given you authority to trample on snakes and scorpions and to overcome all the power of the enemy; nothing will harm you."

This authority isn't about arrogance—it's about alignment. It means standing firm in God's promises and refusing to let fear dictate my actions.

I began to declare God's Word over my life. When doubt tried to creep in, I countered it with truth. I reminded myself that I wasn't walking this journey alone—God was with me, strengthening me every step of the way.

Embracing the Journey

One of the most important lessons I've learned is that the journey of faith isn't always easy, but it's always worth it.

There were moments when I felt like giving up, when the weight of the call felt too heavy. But each time, God reminded me of His faithfulness.

Proverbs 3:5-6 became my guiding light:

"Trust in the Lord with all your heart and lean not on your own understanding; in all your ways submit to him, and he will make your paths straight."

God doesn't expect us to have all the answers. He only asks us to trust Him, take one step at a time, and remain obedient.

Occupying the Promise

Today, I walk in the promises of God with boldness—not because of who I am, but because of who He is.

I am no longer the woman who shrinks back in fear.

I am the woman who steps forward in faith.

And so are you.

God has called you to occupy the land He has promised. Whatever giants stand in your way—fear, doubt, insecurity—know that they are no match for the God who fights for you.

Step into your calling. Trust His plan. Occupy the promise with boldness, knowing that He is with you every step of the way.

A Prayer for Boldness and Dominion

Kind Father, in Jesus' Name,

Before we ask You for anything, we thank You for everything. Thank You for Your love, grace, and the privilege to be called by You. Lord, we thank You for the promises You have spoken over our lives and for the authority You have given us to walk in dominion.

Forgive us for the times we have allowed fear and doubt to hold us back. Today, we choose to trust You completely. We surrender our insecurities and step forward in faith, knowing that You have equipped us for every good work.

Empower us, Lord, to take authority over every lie of the enemy. Strengthen our hearts to walk boldly in the identity You have given us. Lead us by Your Spirit, guide our steps, and remind us that Your presence goes with us wherever we go.

We declare that we are more than conquerors through Christ. We stand firm on Your promises, knowing that no weapon formed against us shall prosper. Lord, we choose to occupy the land You have given us, walking in power, love, and a sound mind.

In Jesus' strong name, we pray. Amen.

Dr. Shavona's Acknowledgements

I honor the legacy of my grandparents Rev. Dr. Walter and Lady Irma Bronson. Without the seeds that they planted in me and the example they lived in front of me, I would not have the spiritual foundation to occupy destiny and purpose. I will forever be there living legacy.

Meet
Dr. Shavona L. Whitehead, BS, MDIV, DMIN

Dr. Shavona L. Whitehead, a native of Maryland, holds a Bachelor of Science degree in Management from Coppin State University, a Master of Divinity degree from Wesley Theological Seminary, and an earned Doctor of Ministry degree in Social and Environmental Justice from Interdenominational Theological Center and Morehouse School of Religion.

Dr. Whitehead, affectionately called Dr. Von, is known as *The MORE Pusher.* She is an ordained preacher, certified life and empowerment coach, and trained spiritual chaplain from Johns Hopkins Hospital. As *The MORE Pusher*, she creates spaces and experiences where women can encounter holistic healing that ignites wholeness.

Dr. Whitehead was ordained under the Pentecostal Reformation in May 2006 and later reaffirmed under the Baptist denomination in May 2015 under the leadership of her maternal grandfather and pastor, the late Rev. Dr. Walter Bronson, Jr. Under his nurturing, her spiritual gifts were developed. Hearing the voice of God, she remains submitted to the pastoral and prophetic covering of Pastor Kenneth Flight, Jr. under Bishop Christopher Windley.

She is the Founder and Chief Executive Officer of Dr. Shavona Whitehead, LLC, and The MORE Experience, which she established in 2020. *MORE: Motivated Overcomers being Restored and Empowered* is a movement dedicated to healing and wholeness. She helps individuals break free from cycles of traumatic chaos and show up as their authentic selves. Her programs guide women to unpack their whole being—spiritually, emotionally, physically, and mentally. Through her unique MORE model, which blends empowerment, transparency, and spiritual impartation, she has transformed the lives of individuals, groups, communities, and families worldwide.

Dr. Whitehead's mission has always been to fulfill God's will by spreading the gospel of Jesus Christ across nations. While teaching others about Christ, she has served in various leadership capacities in both ministry and the marketplace. Her calling has led her to serve and travel to London, St. Thomas, and Brazil, as well as throughout the United States, sharing the gospel. She continues to refine her knowledge and spiritual gifts through ongoing training to ensure that her impact in both the kingdom and the world remains transformative.

She is the published author of *I Am More Now: Empowerment Journal* and her sophomore book, *The Cutting That Made Me Whole*, as well as a contributing author in numerous internationally recognized best-selling works. Her journey of overcoming pain and circumstances has fueled her belief that her story is someone else's breakthrough. Her mantra, *"My Journey Is Someone's Freedom,"* has propelled her forward, leading to features in various digital network publications, billboards in Atlanta and New York, and appearances on major radio, television, and newspaper outlets.

Dr. Whitehead is a proud member of Zeta Phi Beta Sorority, Incorporated, an organization deeply rooted in sisterhood, scholarship, service, and finer womanhood. Being part of this esteemed sisterhood has allowed her to forge lifelong friendships and make a meaningful impact on the world around her. She actively supports the organization's mission through community service projects, educational outreach, and social advocacy initiatives.

On kingdom assignment, Dr. Whitehead seeks God for every move, serving as a change agent in both the kingdom and the world. Her commitment is reflected in her annual events, *Restore Your ROAR Experience* and *The THRIVE Chamber Encounter*, as well as her weekly *Lunchtime Empowerment Talks with Dr. Von*. As she continues to pursue her God-given purpose and destiny, she is supported by her loving husband, four children, and countless individuals who have flourished under her leadership.

Contact information:

Website: www.shavonawhitehead.com

Email: info@ shavonawhitehead.com

Social Media : Facebook- Shavona Whitehead and The MORE Experience / Instagram - @ IAmDrVon / YouTube - Dr. Shavona Whitehead / TikTok - IAmDrVon

Carbonado: You Are Stronger Than You Know

By Apostle Dr. Helen R. Aguocha

Introduction:

Many roads have led me to seek and pursue divine knowledge from God about both my natural and spiritual heritage. I firmly believe that the spiritual anatomy of a person is given by His intent and inspiration to fulfill His divine plan and purpose while journeying through this thing called life.

There is nothing more powerful than life's trials—unpleasant encounters and earthly disappointments—to ignite the desire to overcome obstacles. These challenges prove to us that we have incredible sustaining power and that grace rests over our lives, equipping us to endure even the most difficult seasons.

I have come to realize that my spiritual legacy, natural bloodline, and generational blessings are meant to work in my favor. God has granted me the ability to possess the same qualities as a CARBONADO—a rare, unbreakable diamond. I am built to last and endure until the end. No matter what comes my way, I am here to stay. And so are you.

You are stronger than you know! It's time to discover God's will for your life—your purpose and destiny. I was born to be a blessing, and I was born to be blessed. I was created to shine, carrying the unshakable nature of a CARBONADO.

Situation & Occasion

God often uses unwelcome situations and circumstances to reveal truth. In 2010, I received a phone call that was nothing short of an open invitation to do battle on the front lines of ministry. Members of OIMZION were being harassed and terrorized by the devil in their own home. Frankly, they had reached their wits' end with their demon-possessed son. Riddled with fear and anxiety, they called me, desperately seeking help to relieve them from the tormentor by removing him from their household.

Of course, I didn't know where to begin in order to rectify the wrongs that were being carried out by the devil and their son—but God knew exactly what was needed. Upon entering the home, I immediately took authority over the demon and commanded him to sit down and cease verbally attacking his parents. At my command, the devil was silenced, and the young man began to draw on a Big Chief tablet.

I was both amazed and astonished by the vividness and precision of his drawing. The demon sketched an image of a woman wearing a pearl necklace, draped over her heart, with a chain that clasped a large, diamond-shaped pendant resting across her chest. The details were striking—the heart-shaped diamond was positioned exactly where the natural heart would be on a body. Sparkles and brightness radiated from the heart, dominating the entire image.

When I asked the demon what the drawing meant and what it represented, he responded with an eerie calmness. He told me it was a picture of my heart—and that he hated it. He despised it because my heart was a diamond, filled with the presence of the Godhead and everything Heaven stands for.

I don't have to tell you—I immediately broke out into praise, giving thanks to God before proceeding to cast the devil out of the young man. Needless to say, **we all** experienced deliverance that day.

That moment changed me. I realized that the condition of my heart must remain pure and cannot be compromised or influenced by culture. My heart is like a diamond—rare, unbreakable, and unwavering in its duty toward the things of God.

Carbonado Origin

Black diamonds meet the criteria for determining the natural origin of their color due to the natural presence of black particles. Their color is black by nature but has nothing to do with race or skin color. Black diamonds are elements that constitute, legislate, and execute divine orders established by a higher authority and realm. A person who is born of the Spirit and does not focus on the things of the flesh is always in position spiritually to be classified and qualified as a black diamond—a precious stone indeed.

Known as the hardest and most valuable in its class, diamonds symbolize love, wealth, purity, endurance, and covenant. The origin of black diamonds is controversial, with several theories and hypotheses surrounding their existence. Some suggest they were formed through radiation, meteoritic impact, a stellar supernova explosion, or direct conversion. In other words, black diamonds are truly out of this world and are not meant to be fashioned by earthly means.

The Bible declares in Deuteronomy 28:13:

"And the Lord will make you the head, and not the tail; you shall be above only and not beneath, if you heed the commandments of the Lord your God, which I command you today, and are careful to observe them."

We must live according to the word of God! This takes on a whole new meaning when we accept God's will and allow Him to introduce us to the newness of life—represented by the uniqueness of the black diamond.

Black Diamonds: A Reflection of God's Handiwork

Throughout history, many ancient cultures interpreted natural occurrences, extreme weather events, and celestial phenomena as messages from God. Diamonds, particularly black diamonds, can be seen as messages sent from above to communicate the heart and mind of God to the earth. There are countless biblical accounts of supernatural manifestations sent by God, and black diamonds are no exception. They are naturally beautiful, defying human reasoning and scientific explanation.

Black diamonds are indeed cut from a different cloth, possessing a spirit unlike any other. Those who encounter them recognize without a shadow of a doubt that black diamonds reflect God's hand at work in the world. Whether the circumstances surrounding them are public or private, it is evident that God justly rewards those who believe in His divine creation.

Carbonados are unique and unusual polycrystalline diamonds, often regarded as the gemstone of intellect, preventing misunderstandings and fostering clear communication. They counteract confusion and disorder, which are tactics of the enemy. Most black diamonds are found in Central Africa and Brazil, making them extremely rare. The term "carbonado" was coined by Portuguese explorers in Brazil in the mid-18th century, named for its visual resemblance to burned charcoal.

The Spiritual Parallel of a Black Diamond

Individuals who embody the qualities of a black diamond stand out effortlessly—not because of their outward appearance but because of their spiritual qualities. God is interested in the total person—spirit, soul, and body—and desires to use each life for His glory. Our lives should reflect purity, invincibility, and divine purpose.

Diamonds shine the brightest in darkness, though the darkness cannot comprehend their light. In the same way, a black diamond represents commitment, faithfulness, and covenant. It symbolizes brilliance, strength, and immeasurable wisdom. Unlike white diamonds, black diamonds are in a class of their own—referred to as "fancy black diamonds." Yet, regardless of their category, all diamonds are made under intense pressure and formed through extreme conditions.

The Process of Refinement

Pressure—a continuous force that produces transformation upon its subject—is what refines diamonds. Black diamonds, submitted unto God, are His vessels. They are resilient, unshakable, and incapable of being destroyed by the schemes of the enemy. Their strong, enduring nature allows them to thrive even in the most challenging and adverse conditions.

A person who possesses the qualities of a black diamond stands on the unshakable foundation of Jesus Christ. Nothing less will do. The Bible affirms this truth in Matthew 7:24–25:

"Therefore whosoever heareth these sayings of mine, and doeth them, I will liken him unto a wise man, which built his house upon a rock: And the rain descended, and the floods came, and the winds blew, and beat upon that house; and it fell not: for it was founded upon a rock."

Wisdom and knowledge are the portion of those who are deeply rooted in Christ. It takes divine wisdom to navigate life, and those who know their God will remain strong and do great exploits in His name.

The Spiritual Significance of Jewelry

The Bible presents jewelry in a positive light, and I am on a mission to uphold that truth. I delight in the Lord and in the wisdom and revelation He has released regarding the mysteries of Heaven—particularly concerning black diamonds.

Wearing jewelry, especially black diamonds, should be a reflection of one's spiritual health and wealth. It is not about vanity or material gain; rather, it symbolizes the beauty that flows from within. True beauty does not come from external adornments but from the presence of God dwelling within us.

Isaiah 61:10 declares:

"I will greatly rejoice in the Lord, my soul shall be joyful in my God; for he hath clothed me with the garments of salvation, he hath covered me with the robe of righteousness, as a bridegroom decketh himself with ornaments, and as a bride adorneth herself with her jewels."

Black diamonds represent holiness. As we grow closer to God, we develop the beauty of His holiness in our souls. What matters most in life is not our physical appearance but our spiritual condition. Everything we possess and everything we are should inspire us to glorify God and give Him thanks—for He alone is the source of true beauty.

Dr. Helen's Acknowledgments

A special thanks and recognition are in order for my husband, **Prophet Godday Aguocha, "The Commanding Commander,"** and my **OIMZION Church Family.**

As "The Commanding Commander," it is a privilege to know that when I navigate through tough and rough terrain, loving hands hold me up, refusing to let me fall. Even when I face challenges that scream, *sit down and shut up,* I am encouraged to keep standing and shout even louder:

I'M A BLACK DIAMOND—CARBONADO EXTRAORDINAIRE!

Meet
Apostle Dr. Helen R. Aguocha

Apostle Dr. Helen R. Aguocha is a dedicated supporter of her community in Texas, possessing a unique and gifted ability to relate to and contribute to global communities. As an alumna of several accredited universities, Dr. Helen has pursued and achieved various degrees of higher learning, from a Bachelor of Arts to Doctoral programs.

She is the Co-Founder and Pastor of OIMZION International Global Ministries & Missions in Texas, as well as Stream of Life Zion International in Nigeria and other nations. Known as *The Skillful Surgeon*, she is a highly sought-after prophetic ministry gift and apostolic officer, used mightily by the Holy Spirit to usher in change. Her ministry has taken her across national and international borders, including Nigeria, Mexico, Israel, Europe, China, London, India, and Haiti, where she ministers to the needs of God's people.

Dr. Aguocha is recognized as a rare and valuable gift to the Body of Christ, uniquely graced to minister to all people groups. She is widely known for her cutting-edge wisdom and bold approach to revealing truth. As *The Skillful Surgeon*, she operates with precision and excellence in the spiritual realm, making her highly respected in the prophetic and apostolic community. She carries a well-established reputation for prophetic accuracy and apostolic leadership, trusted by many. A *General in God's Army* and *Commanding Commanda*, she is a powerful force on the frontlines of spiritual warfare, bringing transformation through the Holy Spirit.

Accomplishments and Contributions

Dr. Aguocha's extensive impact includes the **Apostolic Faith-Filled Effective Christian Training (A.F.F.E.C.T.)** Leadership Development program, which provides spiritual training and instruction on becoming effective apostolic and prophetic vessels.

She is also a **prolific playwright, dynamic producer of live stage performances, entrepreneur, and business owner**. Her creative projects include:

- **"I Love Food: Soul Series—Christ 'N' Cuisine,"** streaming on YouTube

- **"By Fire or By Force,"** a social media monthly podcast

- **Heavenly Hair Divine Diner**, where she serves as chef and visionary

- **Inventor of Black Diamond Sensation products**, including Liquid Supplement, Rejuvenating Skin Release, and Valiant Vulva

- **Owner of Everything Sales Store**, offering a variety of products for all needs

Dr. Aguocha is also the author of *Black Diamond Sensation: Carbonado—Rare Jewel!* and a firm believer in the statement: *"You are stronger than you know."*

A Spiritual Encounter and the Revelation of the Carbonado

Dr. Aguocha discovered her spiritual heritage in 2010 when she was called to intervene in a household plagued by demonic harassment. Answering their spiritual 911 call, she took authority over the demon, which then began to draw an image of a radiant pearl necklace draped over a heart, with a chain clasping a large, diamond-shaped pendant on a human chest.

When asked about the meaning of the drawing, the demon revealed that it represented Dr. Aguocha's heart—a heart he despised because it shone like a glistening diamond, carrying the fullness of the Godhead. This encounter solidified her belief that her spiritual legacy, natural bloodline, and generational blessings were meant to work in her favor. Over time, she recognized that God had given her the nature of a carbonado, or black diamond—rare, unbreakable, and built to endure. She boldly declares: *"No matter what comes my way, I am here to stay!"*

A Mission to Empower Others

"Carbonado" is dedicated to the countless individuals searching for their God-ordained assignment and purpose in life. Carbonados are diamonds in the rough—rare, impervious, precious, elect, durable, and set apart.

Dr. Aguocha is also the founder and producer of **"Forecast for the Outcast,"** a television broadcast sponsored by a local university media mogul.

Heavenly Hair: A Ministry of Compassion

One of Dr. Helen's most impactful ministries is **Heavenly Hair: "Until There's a Cure…We Provide Comfort,"** a global initiative she established in 2003. With chapters in the USA and Nigeria, this ministry provides a much-needed service to cancer patients and individuals experiencing medical-related hair loss. Recognizing the emotional toll of losing hair due to illness, she created this ministry to help patients regain their self-esteem and confidence.

Wigs and hairpieces are donated free of charge to those undergoing treatments that cause hair loss. OIMZION International Global Ministries & Missions hosts an annual **Heavenly Hair Runway Extravaganza**, featuring models from all walks of life, to raise awareness and celebrate this ministry.

Chow for Champions: Feeding the Future

A mother of compassion with the heart of a lion, Dr. Aguocha's desire to serve her community led to the creation of **"Chow for Champions,"** a food program providing free nutritional meals to children up to 18 years old, year-round. She is dedicated to helping young people reach beyond their current circumstances by first meeting their basic needs.

For the past ten years, she has also spearheaded memorial scholarships to support high school graduates in their pursuit of higher education.

Apostolic General: A Proven Leader in Spiritual Warfare

Apostle Dr. Helen R. Aguocha has spent her life doing battle on the frontlines of ministry. Her legacy as an Apostolic General and fearless leader is undeniable. Through her work in both local and global communities, she continues to demonstrate infallible proof that she is indeed a God-sent carbonado—unshakable, enduring, and rare.

Occupy Until He Returns

By Dr. Annette Watson-Johnson, M.A., B.S.

Luke 19:11-13 – Jesus Tells His Servants to "Occupy" Until He Returns

In the Bible, "occupy" means to be active and to do the work of the Lord. It also means using one's time, talents, and resources for God's purpose. Occupying is not about being passive or just listening— it is about taking action in our faith. The word also means to be engaged, to stay busy, or to "carry on business by trading."

But how can we occupy when we lack the energy, focus, desire, or discernment to do God's work? How do we remain engaged when life drains us? We can all start by making small but powerful shifts in our daily lives, creating an atmosphere where God can use us.

Reclaiming Our Crowns

Many of us, Black women and men, have self-crowned ourselves as "Queens" and "Kings" without ever stepping foot in a pageant or having a physical crown placed upon our heads. We claim these titles because, deep down, we know our worth. We are the descendants of Africans with royal lineage, yet we were the first to be sold into slavery. The legacy of our ancestors manifests in our spiritual and psychological resilience. Hence the phrase, "I get it from my momma."

Much of our history has been erased, rewritten, or buried, but who is to say that we are not royalty? Despite enduring some of the worst human atrocities, we rise. That strength, that divine power, is woven into our DNA. But when we call ourselves Queens or Kings, we must honor our crowns. We must know our strengths, our value, and our purpose so that we can move forward with clarity and focus.

It doesn't matter whether your crown is visible or invisible—what matters is that you carry it with dignity. As we step into 2025, here are five ways to adjust our crowns and walk with purpose.

1. Readjust Your Crown

To readjust means to adapt to a changed environment or situation. In 2025 and beyond, the atmosphere has shifted. We are all aware of the **outcome of the 2024 U.S. election** and what it means for us. This is not the time for distractions.

Be still and move in silence. No more wasted energy on protests, marches, or international concerns that do not directly affect us. We must be laser-focused on ourselves, our immediate families, and the things that matter most.

- **Let go of ungrateful family members** who take advantage of your time, space, and finances. Some people believe that no matter how old they get, you are supposed to provide for them simply because they are family. You are not obligated to carry their weight.

- **Stop overextending yourself at work.** We work overtime, make the best recommendations, spearhead extracurricular projects, and still manage to carry our own workload—yet we are often overlooked for promotions, pay raises, and recognition. In 2025, work within your job description and save your best energy for your own growth.

- **Distance yourself from toxic relationships.** Whether it's a friend or a romantic partner, if they constantly drain you with negativity and selfishness, it's time to set boundaries.

As Queens and Kings, we can no longer tolerate disrespect from anyone. We must make the decision to stop enabling those who act like leeches. We must take charge of our own time, peace, and purpose.

So, ask yourself: What will your crown represent in 2025? Will it symbolize wisdom, discipline, and self-respect—or will it reflect exhaustion, burnout, and misplaced loyalty?

The choice is yours. **Occupy your space. Adjust your crown. Walk in your power.**

2. Maintain a Close Relationship with God

This is where our strength lies. Staying faithful, prayerful, and thankful will only deepen our relationship with God, our Father. Our faith, discernment, spiritual growth, and biblical knowledge will lead us along the path He has set before us. Each of our journeys is unique, so we should always put God first and trust that He will deliver on His promises.

3. Take Your Health Seriously

I encourage everyone I encounter to listen to their body and what it is telling them. Our bodies warn us when something is not working properly, but too often, we ignore these signs. If certain foods—sweets, pork, dairy—consistently make you feel unwell, then consider reducing or eliminating them from your diet. It's no coincidence that after Easter, Thanksgiving, and Christmas, the church prayer lists seem to grow longer.

God called me into the Wellness Ministry after I was on the verge of a mental breakdown. When He healed me, He led me to start Dynamic Participators Enterprises Inc., a non-profit organization that allows me to use my testimony to consult and educate others. In this organization, we emphasize that mental, physical, and spiritual health are interconnected and must be incorporated into all aspects of our daily lives.

We support this holistic approach through professional consultations, motivational workshops, community outreach, virtual events, youth mentoring, and various educational resources. We also collaborate with churches, non-profits, federal organizations, local schools, and community initiatives. As our company grows, we remain committed to adapting to new data and the evolving needs of those we serve.

God still wasn't finished with me. In 2019, I had a dream where I heard Him say, "Just Get Well." I didn't immediately understand the meaning, so I reached out to my daughter, parents, and siblings for their insight. They all advised me to let God lead.

That's when He directed me into my kitchen, revealing to me the gift of herbalism. I became deeply intrigued by the healing properties of sea moss and began formulating my own product line, Just Get Well Sea Moss. When the COVID-19 pandemic struck in 2020, I realized exactly what God had been preparing me for.

As an advocate for wellness, I knew it was my responsibility to educate others on the benefits of natural healing. I launched marketing efforts, shared information, and created products tailored to the needs of my family and community. In obedience to God's call, I expanded my vision through Dynamic AWJ Products LLC, which now produces over 55 organic, plant-based, vegan, and cruelty-free wellness products.

These products are beneficial for all, but my primary focus remains on the Black community, where generational health issues persist due to long-standing oppression and lack of access to proper resources. My product line includes sea moss gels, capsules, herbal teas, creams, oils, and body care essentials designed for both internal and external healing.

God gave me a clear understanding: He created us from the dust of the earth, and we must nourish our bodies with what He has provided.

We rely too much on mass-produced foods, synthetic medicines, and chemically-altered body care products. As a result, our bodies are undernourished, deficient, and increasingly vulnerable to disease. Genetically modified and bioengineered foods have created a cycle of dependency that has kept us sick.

We must place more trust in God's medicine—plant-based foods and natural healing remedies. We are no longer slaves; we don't have to eat the scraps of the past. We have the power to make better choices. Yes, we have been freed from forced labor, but we have shifted our dependency to the pharmaceutical industry, making others rich at the expense of our own health.

Think about that. Now that we know better, let's do better.

4. Live Your Life Like It's Golden

Reinvest your time, energy, and efforts back into yourself. If you work hard, you should also take the time to enjoy life. Stay off the front lines of every battle, and stop prioritizing national, international, or local concerns that do not serve you.

The results of the 2024 U.S. election should have made one thing clear: our input and support of democracy are not appreciated. From the moment our ancestors were taken from Africa and forced into slavery, Black women have carried the weight of being nurturers, caretakers, providers, and protectors. Despite being the most imitated and admired, we are also the most disrespected.

Yes, we are the chosen people according to the Bible, but even God allows for rest. It is time to take a step back and focus on ourselves. When we shift our focus from external distractions to internal growth, we will clearly see the vision God has for us.

5. Mind Your Black-Owned Businesses

Due to systemic racism and financial suppression, Black-owned businesses often struggle to thrive. Many, like mine, are self-funded, relying on residual income and reinvestment from business profits rather than external financial support.

If you can afford to, make it a priority to support at least one Black-owned business each month. This is especially important now, as federal and non-profit programs that once provided funding for minority-owned businesses are being challenged or eliminated altogether.

When choosing where to spend your money, support businesses that respect your time, appreciate your patronage, and uphold dignity in their interactions. This is a common discussion within our community, and it's time we take action.

We must do better to ensure our businesses remain competitive, sustainable, and impactful.

Occupy Until He Comes

To occupy means to stay engaged in the work of the Kingdom until Jesus returns. This is not the time for complacency, nor is it the time for distractions. We must be intentional in all we do—our faith, our health, our relationships, and our economic power.

Ask yourself:

- What does my life represent?

- How am I protecting my energy, my health, and my purpose?

- Am I truly occupying the place God has prepared for me?

It's time to rise up, readjust, and walk boldly into the next season. The world is shifting, but God's promises remain. Occupy until He comes.

To occupy is to engage in Kingdom business until He returns, not disengage in escapism biding our time.

Dr. Annette's Acknowledgments

First, all praises to God for gifting me. I want to thank Him for giving me discernment and the obedience to follow His direction. I am grateful for the way He speaks to me in my dreams, for blessing me with the gift of premonition, and for guiding me in every step of my journey.

I extend my deepest thanks to my late parents, John and Addie Watson, for ensuring that my siblings and I were prepared for whatever life would bring our way. Their wisdom, love, and resilience laid the foundation for who I am today.

To my children, Provine Cosby Jr. and Octavia Cosby—you are my biggest cheerleaders. Your love, encouragement, and unwavering belief in me continue to inspire me to push forward and pursue my purpose.

To my family and friends, your support is endless, and I am beyond grateful for the love you show me.

And I cannot forget my countless customers who share their powerful testimonials, encouraging others to use my Just Get Well Sea Moss products. Your stories of transformation and healing bring me so much joy. I love and appreciate you all!

Dr. Annette Watson-Johnson

Annette Watson-Johnson was born in St. Louis, MO, but currently resides in Florida. She was blessed with an honorary Doctorate Degree in Christian University from the United Bible Christian University of London, England. She is a graduate of National University of California, where she earned her Master of Arts in Human Resource Management. She is also an alumnus of the University of Maryland, where she earned her Bachelor of Science in Business Management and an Associate of Arts in Business Administration.

She is the CEO and founder of Dynamic Participators Enterprise Inc., a non-profit organization, and the founder of AWJ Products LLC, which houses her Girls Run the World in Pearls projects, book self-publishing services, and the Just Get Well Sea Moss product line.

Annette has been an Amazon Best-Selling Author 11 times and is also a motivational and international speaker, as well as a wellness ambassador.

For booking inquiries, speaking engagements, sea moss wellness consultations, or to support Annette, she can be reached through various communication channels and social media platforms listed below.

Mind Space

By Tyesha Cannon

Everything we engage in begins with our mindset. While we can't always control our thoughts, actively renewing our minds is essential for healthy thinking and living.

"And do not be conformed to this world, but be transformed by the renewing of your mind, that you may prove what is that good and acceptable and perfect will of God." (Romans 12:2 NKJV)

To cultivate a mental space filled with positivity and the teachings of Christ Jesus, we must deliberately choose what we allow to reside within. Our minds are powerful; they send messages to our bodies, influencing our thinking, speaking, and movement. But what happens when we drift through life, believing without purpose and speaking without intention? Our words can become empty, falling by the wayside, and leaving our brilliant ideas and dreams as unrealized potential.

I don't know about you, but that is a risk I am **NOT** willing to take!

It is time to take back our minds in the name of Jesus and embrace a new mindset!

The Power of Repetition

Have you ever heard the saying *"practice makes progress"*? Well, I want you to know "This includes the concept of repetition. Repetition is crucial for learning, developing habits, and creating new thinking pathways. Progression takes the pressure of perfection off of us. When we practice something consistently, it becomes second nature.

This is why hiding God's Word in our hearts and minds must be intentional. It is not enough to be a hearer only—we must also be doers of His Word. Our commitment to God should be unwavering—free from doubt or negotiation. However, when intrusive thoughts come we have access to God requesting for his help. (Hebrews 4:16 NKJV) Our yes to God must evolve into a genuine and sincere *"yes"*—a declaration we not only speak but also live out. Our *"yes"* is a form of worship to God. Tasha Cobbs Leonard once said on The Jennifer Hudson Show, "I say yes to God before I can logically say No."

This mindset reflects clarity and a determined spirit that remains steadfast against fear, doubt, and uncertainty, with a yielding spirit to what the Lord wants for our lives. A person with strong convictions cannot be easily swayed. They make use of their inner voice to fight against counter thoughts that do not align with God's truth, taking every thought captive and making it obedient to Christ while outwardly demonstrating this through the power of prayer.

"Casting down imaginations, and every high thing that exalteth itself against the knowledge of God, and bringing into captivity every thought to the obedience of Christ." (2 Corinthians 10:5 KJV)

Embracing a Transformative Mindset

To truly embrace the mindset of Christ, we must fill our thoughts, mouth, eyes, and ears with God's wisdom and heavenly perspective through the Word of God. When we center our minds on Jesus, we gain clarity and purpose that points us toward a more fulfilling life.

Will our flesh resist? Absolutely.

Never forget that the flesh will never agree with the Spirit—they are always in conflict, at war with one another. The question is: **who will you allow to win?**

You have the power to make a conscious decision. There will be moments when you may not *feel* inclined to obey God, but it is in these moments that your faith activates, bringing immense joy and pleasure to the Almighty King.

A mind and heart that pleases God is a space occupied by His word, love, and purpose!

"Let this mind be in you which was also in Christ Jesus." Philippians 2:5 NKJV

The Mind is the Battlefield:

Even though the victory has already been won through Christ Jesus, He never promised that we wouldn't have to fight battles. In fact, **your mind is the number one battlefield for warfare**, and the enemy knows this. When our minds are overwhelmed with uncontrollable thoughts, distressing experiences, and wicked imaginations, after we have prayed for hours, days, and even nights without finding relief, we need to develop strategies to clear our **mental space** and reclaim the peace that belongs to us in Christ Jesus. While there are times when we may need to cast out demonic spirits, it's essential to take a practical approach to our deliverance as well. We must remember that demons often attempt to return, sometimes increasing in number and creating stronger influences, which can intensify their stronghold. *(mentioned in Matthew 12:43-45 NKJV)* **Therefore, we should shift our mindset by developing new thinking patterns and combining them with action. By doing this it creates new and improved cycles resulting in a changed mindset, transforming what seems impossible into the Possible!**

Strategies for Clearing Your Mind Space

- **Identify what is living rent-free in your mind.** What thoughts are occupying your mind space without your permission? Such as Fear, anxiety, depression, suicidal thoughts, regret, rejection, loneliness, unhealthy people-pleasing, or financial struggles?

Recognizing these intruders is the first step to evicting them.

- **Incorporate prayer, fasting, reading God's Word, fellowship, and worship.**

  Include God in your daily routine, especially in moments of mental battles. When you fill your mind with His presence, there is no room for the enemy's lies. They can come, but they won't stay. Allow the Holy Spirit to lead and guide you for you are not alone; you have the help of the Lord, but it is recognized in those quiet moments of stillness.

- **Then will come joy.**

  "His favor is for life; weeping may endure for a night, but joy comes in the morning." (Psalm 30:5 NKJV) No season lasts forever—seasons are meant to change,

and so must we. We need to have stored-up prayers in preparation for those changing seasons. Morning brings joy, so start your day with prayer and gratitude. Find joy in God's presence. Listen for the Holy Spirit to speak to you. Keep a journal to document these powerful moments of breakthrough and transformation.

"You will show me the path of life; in Your presence is fullness of joy; at Your right hand are pleasures forevermore." (Psalm 16:11 NKJV)

Lasting joy and strength can only be found in God's presence. His presence provides what the world **cannot**—peace, security, and unwavering love.

Do Not Let Unwanted Thoughts Become Your Reality

The thoughts that enter your mind do not have to take root. Cast them **immediately** upon the One who cares for you.

- *"Pour out all your worries and stress upon Him and leave them there, for He always tenderly cares for you."* (1 Peter 5:7 TPT)

- *"Be anxious for nothing, but in everything by prayer and supplication, with thanksgiving, let your requests be made known to God; and the peace of God, which surpasses all understanding, will guard your hearts and minds through Christ Jesus."* (Philippians 4:6-7 NKJV)

Pause and Reflect in Gratitude

Take a moment to express heartfelt gratitude to God for the incredible gifts He provides:

- His **profound peace**, which washes over us and brings comfort in times of trouble.

- His **deliverance**, which frees us from struggles and burdens.

- His **restoration**, which brings healing and renewal to our souls (mind, will, and emotions).

- His **constant presence**, which surrounds us, reminding us that we are never alone.

- His **unconditional love**, which enriches our lives in ways we often take for granted.

Let us celebrate the safety and security we find in Him, knowing that **in His presence, we are made whole.**

All the Joys of Thanksgiving

"Let us come before His presence with thanksgiving; let us shout joyfully to Him with psalms." (Psalm 95:2 NKJV)

Thanksgiving brings a renewed sense of energy. It lifts your spirit and inspires you to express gratitude from deep within. Instead of focusing on concerns, you shift to thanking God for all He has done in your life. You begin to remember who God is—the Almighty, the Sovereign One—and in doing so, you gain confidence in your identity as His creation.

As Psalm 139:14 (NKJV) reminds us, *"I will praise You, for I am fearfully and wonderfully made; marvelous are Your works, and my soul knows very well."* From this place of remembrance, we thank Him—not only for the significant moments in life but for the consistent and future blessings as well.

Thanksgiving is an expression of faith! You begin to thank God for your now, and in advance for what you believe is coming. The Holy Spirit reminds you of God's goodness and the fresh mercy and compassion He provides every morning. Even every breath you take is an act of praise, a reminder that your very existence glorifies Him.

"It is of the LORD's mercies that we are not consumed because His compassions fail not. They are new every morning: Great is Thy faithfulness." (Lamentations 3:22-23 KJV)

A thankful heart **clears your mind** and reassures you that God is more than enough. He will never lead you astray.

"Trust in the Lord with all your heart, and lean not on your own understanding; in all your ways acknowledge Him, and He shall direct your paths." (Proverbs 3:5-6 NKJV)

Refreshing the Mind Space

When we declutter our minds and clear the space, we allow God's thoughts to fill the void. This mental renewal brings a fresh flow of thinking, realigning our focus with what is praiseworthy and rooted in God's love.

"Finally, brethren, whatever things are true, whatever things are noble, whatever things are just, whatever things are pure, whatever things are lovely, whatever things are of a good report, if there is any virtue and if there is anything praiseworthy—meditate on these things. The things which you learned and received and heard and saw in me, these do, and the God of peace will be with you." (Philippians 4:8-9 NKJV)

This is the mental upgrade you've been waiting for—one that encourages you to keep moving forward. The world needs you, but how can you effectively do God's work with a distracted mind?

It simply won't work.

It's time to remain active until Christ returns for His Church. His people need restoration, and God has given us assignments to complete. But He will first work in us before He works through us.

Distraction prevents traction, resulting in no productive action.

However, when you decide to start again, you experience a renewed mindset, and everything you've endured along the way paves the path for God's glorious revelation.

Consider what God is calling you to do. Much of your purpose is reflected in what you have gone through. God will use your journey to help you recognize your community—the people He has assigned you to guide into a new beginning, leaving the past behind, and also the people who are assigned to you for your personal release.

It's time to elevate your mindset because the higher you strive to go, the closer you get to God. When God's hand is upon your life, you become untouchable.

Success looks different for everyone, but at its core, it is always tied to your willingness and obedience to God. You will achieve everything God has destined for you.

Moving Forward in Faith

Take it one day at a time. Trying to tackle everything at once can be overwhelming. One of my former pastors once preached, *"Think about some things, but pray about everything."*

When you pray, you shift your focus away from yourself and onto the one true living God, who is so great we can't even fathom.

Continue to walk by faith, not by sight. Some things won't come to you right away, but keep speaking the Word of God until His promises become tangible in your life.

You have the opportunity to be the one who starts something that others will follow. God is calling you to break new ground, to take on something rooted in longevity. But you must have faith. You can't please God without it.

God is asking you to achieve something unprecedented in your family history—leaving a legacy that will bless future generations.

This is the inheritance that produces generational blessings.

You are a pioneer.

A trailblazer.

Chosen for greatness.

Destined to be victorious.

You must keep the faith—it is your substance!

Faith is for Now, and Hope is for your Future!

"Now faith is the substance of things hoped for, the evidence of things not seen. For by it the elders obtained a good testimony." (Hebrews 11:1-2 NKJV)

I encourage you to read and study all of Hebrews 11. As you meditate on this chapter, picture yourself facing a challenge that has never been attempted in your lifetime, your bloodline, or your generation.

Imagine how the uncertainty of the unknown may stir up emotions, yet still, your Faith is fueled by God's Word coming to pass.

"So shall My word be that goes forth from My mouth; It shall not return to Me void, But it shall accomplish what I please, And it shall prosper in the thing for which I sent it." (Isaiah 55:11 NKJV)

Just as God's Word moves forward without the option of looking back, so will your work.

When you are no longer here on earth, your legacy will still speak!

It shall go from generation to generation.

Meditation brings Manifestation:

"This Book of the Law shall not depart from your mouth, but you shall meditate in it day and night, that you may observe to do according to all that is written in it. For then you will make your way prosperous, and then you will have good success." (Joshua 1:8 NKJV)

Now is the time to boldly advance in the Kingdom. The Word of God will ignite your journey toward divine success, revealing the true victor within you. Through your willingness and obedience, you will experience the abundant blessings of the land.

"If you are willing and obedient, you shall eat the good of the land." (Isaiah 1:19 NKJV)

I hope you feel inspired and encouraged to occupy yourself, make the most of your time until Christ Jesus returns, and fulfill your God-given purpose and destiny here on earth. May your mind be clear, transparent, and open to receiving new and improved ideas rooted in God's Word.

Remember, **you are not alone—God is always with you.**

Tyesha's Acknowledgments

I want to take a moment to express my heartfelt gratitude to my Lord and Savior, Christ Jesus, for His endless love and guidance in my life. His presence has been a constant source of light, strength and encouragement.

I am profoundly thankful to my parents, **Elders Tyron and Gwendolyn Erskin**. Their loving support and wisdom have provided me with a solid foundation upon which I continue to build my life. Their teachings and values have shaped who I am today.

To the love of my life, **Thomas Michael Cannon**, and our four beautiful children, I cannot thank you enough for your continuous encouragement and love. You are my rock, and your faith in me fuels my passion to pursue my dreams. Our family moments are treasures that I cherish deeply.

I also want to acknowledge our wonderful new church family at **Moriah City of Miracles**. Our shared faith, community, and fellowship have enriched my spiritual journey and provided a supportive network that lifts us all.

Lastly, I would like to extend my heartfelt thanks to **Dr. Kishma**. Your dedication to creating remarkable opportunities for us to fulfill God's purpose is truly inspiring. Thank you for being a **purpose pusher** and for fearlessly saying *"yes"* to God. Your support is invaluable, and I want you to know that it will never go unnoticed.

I love you all dearly!

Meet
Tyesha Cannon

Tyesha Cannon's journey is a powerful testament to the transformative power of faith and dedication. Growing up as a *preacher's kid* in a family deeply rooted in spiritual leadership, her early exposure to the church and its teachings laid the foundation for her profound relationship with God. From experiencing the Holy Spirit at the tender age of five to re-dedicating her life to Christ during a transformative period of teenage pregnancy at 16, Tyesha's story is one of resilience, redemption, and unshakable faith.

Her commitment to living by example and encouraging others to embrace their potential in Christ is evident in her life's work. Tyesha's transparency about her journey—from a teenage mother to a *reborn virgin* and ultimately to a blessed marriage—reflects her deep belief in waiting on the Lord and living a life of purity.

As the Founder, Visionary, and C.E.O. of She Sacred Ministries, LLC, Tyesha has wholeheartedly embraced her calling. Through her ministry, she has passionately spread the gospel, using her fiery testimony to inspire and uplift others. Her impact has reached international platforms, establishing her as a recognized author, speaker, and influencer in the Christian community. Her accolades, including being named one of the Top 30 Influential Women by *K.I.S.H. Magazine*, one of the Top 10 Global Influential Women, and History's Builders: Top Purpose Pushers by *Gleaming Dreamers Magazine*, and receiving the Strong Girl Trophy Award by Prophetess Margaret Green, highlights her growing influence and relentless dedication.

Tyesha's service in the local and global church further demonstrates her deep commitment to faith and community. Over the years, she has served in various roles, including prayer team member, praise dance instructor, praise and worship leader, and marriage ministry director alongside her husband. Now an ordained minister, she continues to be a guiding force in the Church and beyond.

Her personal life is a reflection of God's blessings. Married to her loving husband, Thomas Michael Cannon, and a devoted mother to four wonderful children, Tyesha beautifully balances family, ministry, and professional pursuits. Her commitment to education is evident in her studies in psychology at Maryville University, equipping her with the knowledge to further help others. Additionally, her role as a "Traveling Teacher" for the Special School District demonstrates her passion for education and service, ensuring that every child, regardless of circumstance, receives the support they need to thrive.

Tyesha Cannon's life is a testament to the power of love, faith, repentance, forgiveness, resilience, dedication, and service. Her story is an inspiration—reminding us that, through Christ, we can overcome anything, follow our dreams, serve others, and live a purposeful life anchored in God's Word.

Tyesha Cannon

Founder/ Visionary/C.E.O of She Sacred Ministries, LLC.

Email: shesacredministries@gmail.com

Follow her on social media outlets:

Facebook: Tyesha Cannon

Instagram and YouTube: @tyesha_theencourager

Occupy the Present: The Power of Contentment

By Ayanna Lynnay

We spend so much of our lives looking back or looking ahead that we often miss the beauty of where we are right now. The past is over—it cannot be undone, rewritten, or relived. The future is in God's hands—it is not for us to control, predict, or rush into. Yet, how often do we allow regret over what was and anxiety over what could be to rob us of the peace and joy of where we are right now?

I have learned that **contentment is not complacency**. It is not about settling for less or ignoring the desire for growth. Instead, it is about *accepting where God has placed us today*, knowing that He is sovereign over our past, present, and future. True contentment is not based on external circumstances but on the internal assurance that God is with us *right here, right now.*

The Bible reminds us in Philippians 4:11-13, "I have learned in whatever state I am, to be content. I know how to be abased, and I know how to abound. Everywhere and in all things I have learned both to be full and to be hungry, both to abound and to suffer need. I can do all things through Christ who strengthens me."

Paul understood something that many of us struggle with—contentment is *learned*. It does not come naturally, and it certainly is not the product of a life free from difficulties. Paul had experienced hardship, suffering, and loss, yet he still declared that he had *learned* to be content. If Paul had to learn contentment, so do we.

Letting Go of Yesterday

One of the biggest obstacles to contentment is living in regret over the past. We replay mistakes in our minds, wish we had made different choices, or long for times that we felt were better than where we are now. The enemy loves to keep us bound in regret because as long as we are looking backward, we cannot move forward.

Isaiah 43:18-19 tells us, "Do not remember the former things, nor consider the things of old. Behold, I will do a new thing, now it shall spring forth; shall you not know it?"

God is always doing something new in our lives, but we will not see it if we are fixated on the past. The truth is, everything that has happened up to this point has shaped us, but it does not define us. God does. His plan for our lives was never derailed by our mistakes or failures. He is not pacing the floors of heaven worried about what we should have done differently. He is still in control.

If we truly believe that God is working all things together for our good (Romans 8:28), then we have to trust that even our past failures, missteps, and disappointments are being used to shape us into who He created us to be.

Refusing to Be Anxious About Tomorrow

Just as regret keeps us stuck in the past, **anxiety keeps us fearful about the future**. We live in a culture that is always pushing us toward the next thing—the next goal, the next success, the next opportunity. While there is nothing wrong with ambition, there is a danger in being so focused on what's next that we neglect where we are.

Jesus addressed this directly in Matthew 6:34 when He said, "Therefore do not worry about tomorrow, for tomorrow will worry about its own things. Sufficient for the day is its own trouble."

Worrying about the future does not change it—it only steals today's peace. How many of us have spent sleepless nights worrying about things that never even happened? How much time have we wasted being frustrated because we were not where we *thought* we should be by now?

God is not in a rush. He is not bound by our timelines or deadlines. He knows exactly when and how things will unfold in our lives, and when we truly trust Him, we can rest in that.

Embracing the Gift of Now

One of the greatest revelations I have had is that *today* is a gift. This moment, right here, is a blessing. No matter what it looks like, no matter what we are facing, there is something to be grateful for. When we learn to embrace the present, we unlock the joy and peace that have been available to us all along.

Psalm 118:24 says, "This is the day that the Lord has made; we will rejoice and be glad in it."

Not yesterday. Not tomorrow. **This day.**

What would happen if we truly rejoiced in *this* day? If we stopped waiting for everything to be perfect before we allowed ourselves to be happy? If we stopped saying, *"I'll be happy when..."* and started saying, *"I am grateful now."*

Contentment is about appreciating the *season* you are in, even if it is not where you thought you would be. It is about trusting that God is just as present here as He will be there—wherever *there* is.

Practical Ways to Occupy the Present

1. **Practice Gratitude Daily**

   Instead of focusing on what is missing, focus on what is present. Every day, write down three things you are grateful for. It shifts your perspective from lack to abundance.

2. **Limit Social Media Comparisons**

   One of the biggest thieves of contentment is comparison. The highlight reels of others can make us feel like our own lives are lacking. Remember, God's plan for *you* is unique. You are not behind. You are right where He wants you.

3. **Celebrate Small Wins**

   Sometimes we overlook progress because we are waiting for something big. Celebrate every step forward, no matter how small. It all counts.

4. **Set Goals but Trust God's Timing**

   There is nothing wrong with having goals, but surrender them to God. Work toward them with diligence but **hold them loosely**, allowing God to direct your steps.

5. **Engage Fully in the Present Moment**

   Spend time with loved ones without distraction. Enjoy simple moments. Take in the beauty of where you are.

Sometimes the greatest joys are found in the things we overlook.

6. Surrender Your Worries in Prayer

When anxiety about the future creeps in, take it to God in prayer. Philippians 4:6 reminds us to be anxious for nothing but to bring everything to God with thanksgiving. When we do, His peace guards our hearts and minds.

7. Trust That Delays Are Not Denials

Just because something has not happened yet does not mean it never will. Sometimes, God is preparing us for what we are praying for. Instead of growing frustrated, ask Him, *"What are You teaching me in this season?"*

Living in Fullness Right Now

God is not waiting for us to get to a certain place in life before He starts moving. He is moving right now. His presence is here, His grace is here, His purpose for us in *this season* is here.

We do not have to wait to be happy. We do not have to wait to be at peace. We do not have to wait to feel fulfilled. We can embrace joy, peace, and purpose right now.

Let's stop looking so far ahead that we miss what God is doing in the present. Let's stop carrying regrets that Jesus has already freed us from. Let's stop measuring our success by the world's standards and start seeing our worth through God's eyes.

This moment, right now, is part of the story God is writing. It is not a wasted chapter. It is not a delay. It is part of the process. And if we learn to occupy the present, fully trusting that God is with us here, we will walk into the future with peace, knowing that He has been in control all along.

Wherever you are today, be there fully. Be present. Be grateful. Be at peace. Because just as much as what is ahead.

Ayanna's Acknowledgments'

My Lord and Savior Jesus. I am so thankful for you love, mercy and grace. Where would I be without you? I am soooo glad I don't have to find out. You have given my life meaning and purpose beyond what I could have thought or imagined.

My beautiful daughters **Shakiya and Lauriyana**. I could never thank God enough for allowing me to be you mommy.

My mother Margaret. Thank you for being the best mother me and my sisters Sonya and Melody could have had.

Meet
Ayanna Lynnay

Ayanna Lynnay is a visionary author, speaker, and mentor whose life's mission is to inspire others to step boldly into their God-given purpose. As the founder of ChosenButterfly Publishing, Ayanna has helped many authors bring their stories to life, with many becoming #1 Amazon bestsellers. Through her publishing company and writing courses, she empowers aspiring writers to share their stories with confidence, combining practical tools with faith-based encouragement.

Ayanna is the author of *Devil, Please I Am Still Not Offended,* a powerful book that addresses the damaging effects of offense and equips readers to overcome its grip. She is also the author of *Designed to Dream,* a book that goes beyond simply encouraging big dreams—it reminds readers that they are fully equipped to endure and overcome whatever is necessary to achieve them. Additionally, she wrote the devotional *Seasons Do Change,* which provides spiritual encouragement for navigating life's transitions.

Ayanna is also a co-author in numerous compilation books, contributing her voice and insights across diverse topics such as divorce, starting life over again, faith, purpose, and more. In her writing courses, she integrates the use of AI as a tool to assist writers, making storytelling more accessible and impactful for people at all skill levels. She also teaches courses on how to use AI to help **Kingdom coaches and teachers** build courses and platforms for their audiences, equipping them with the tools to expand their reach and impact.

With a heart rooted in faith, Ayanna is passionate about helping others recognize their potential, trust God through challenges, and embrace the dreams He has placed in their hearts. Whether through her books, teaching, or speaking engagements, Ayanna's message is clear: you are equipped and graced to overcome every obstacle on the path to your destiny.

Ayanna is a wife, mother, and elder at Tabernacle of Praise Buffalo, serving under the leadership of Pastor Charles McCarley. When she's not writing, teaching, or mentoring she enjoys spending time with her family, reading inspiring books, and fostering meaningful connections with others. Her journey is a testament to the power of faith, perseverance, and God's ability to use every step for His glory. Ayanna Lynnay's life and work are dedicated to helping others realize their dreams and live lives of purpose and impact.

If you desire to learn more about becoming a published author or are an aspiring writer looking for assistance, visit <u>ChosenButterflyPublishing.com</u>. Through her courses and services, Ayanna Lynnay and her team are committed to equipping writers with the tools and support needed to bring their stories to life and make an impact.